DENVER MUSEUM OF NATURE & SCIENCE™

The Official Guide

DENVER MUSEUM OF
NATURE & SCIENCE™ | Press

Denver, Colorado

This publication was supported in part by generous grants from A. Reynolds Morse and the Lloyd David and Carlye Cannon Wattis Foundation.

The publisher and author wish to thank the many staff and volunteers who contributed their time and knowledge to this publication.
This book is dedicated to Nancy K. Jenkins.

The Museum's programs and exhibits are made possible in part by funds from the Scientific and Cultural Facilities District.

Project staff
Author: James T. Alton
Project manager: Heidi M. Lumberg
Art director/Designer: Amy L. Thornton
Editor: Pamela Wineman
Photo editor: Nancy K. Jenkins
Media assets coordinator: Kristy Alexander
Media assets intern: Emily Aspenwall
Photo archivist: Liz Clancy

International Standard Book Number: 0-916278-72-7
Library of Congress Catalog Card Number: 00-133344

Published by Denver Museum of Nature and Science Press, 2001 Colorado Boulevard, Denver, Colorado 80205. Printed in China.

Contents

Come Explore

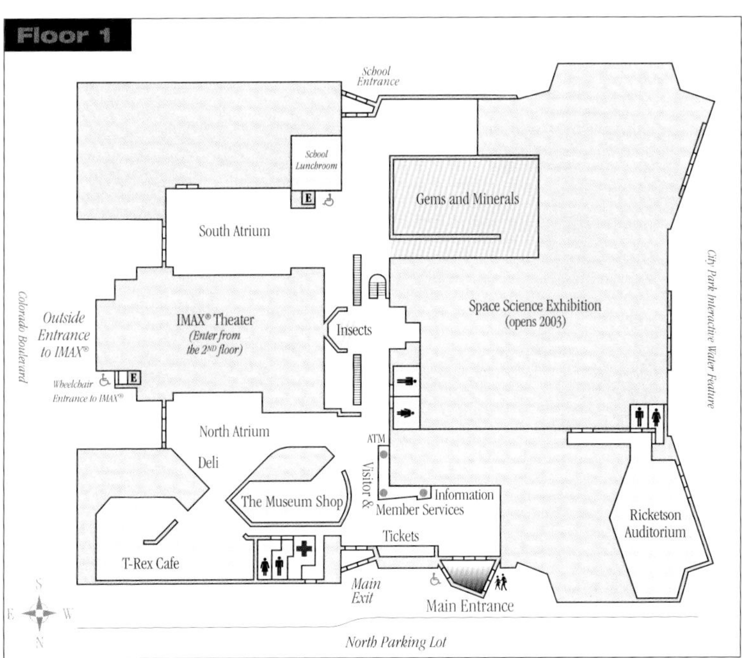

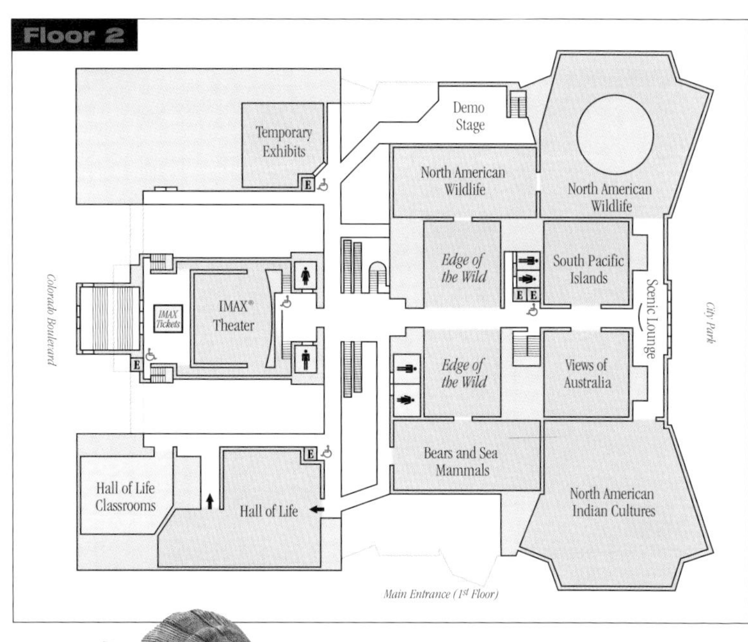

Baskets, shells, and beaded dresses all find a home in our collections.

Floor 3

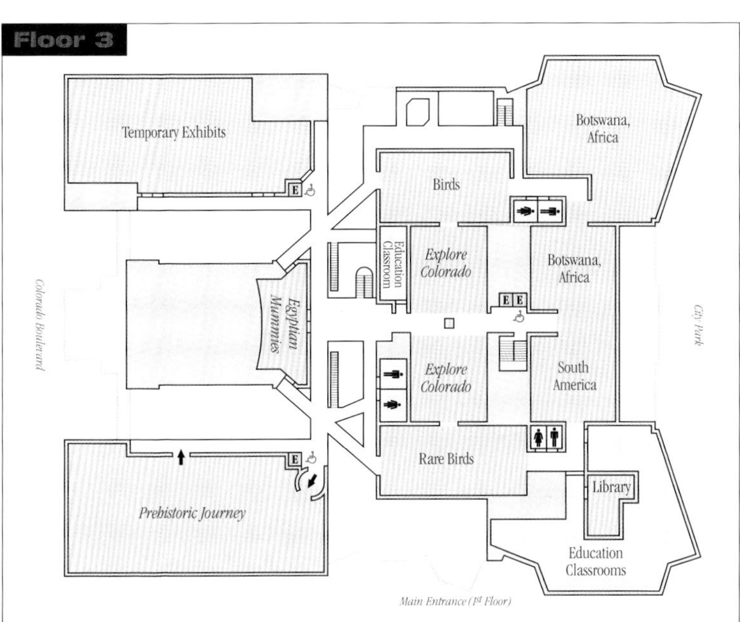

Temporary Exhibits
Botswana, Africa
Birds
Education Classroom
Explore Colorado
Botswana, Africa
Colorado Boulevard
Egyptian Mummies
City Park
Explore Colorado
South America
Rare Birds
Library
Prehistoric Journey
Education Classrooms
Main Entrance (1st Floor)

From the President

Welcome to *Denver Museum of Nature & Science: The Official Guide.* On these pages you will discover the amazingly diverse programs the Museum has to offer—from engaging exhibits to intriguing educational programs to groundbreaking scientific research.

The Denver Museum of Nature and Science boasts a rich 100-year history and has grown to become one of the country's largest natural history museums. As we embark on our second century, we intend to keep the Museum a vibrant work in progress. We will continue to provide exciting learning experiences both inside our building and beyond City Park, building on our role as the Rocky Mountain region's leading resource for informal science education. Through our exhibits and community science programs, people can better understand how science affects their lives. With the world changing at an ever-increasing rate, it is especially important for people of all ages to be scientifically literate. Equipped with such knowledge, we can all contribute to discussing and solving future challenges.

We will also continue to selectively add authentic objects to our collections, because every zoological specimen, Native American basket, or fossil records a part of the world as it exists today or fills in a piece of the past. Each new addition helps our scientists—anthropologists, geologists, space scientists, paleontologists, health scientists, zoologists—decipher the mysteries of the natural world.

Our many programs would not be possible without the generous assistance of individual donors, corporations, and foundations; our talented staff, dedicated volunteers, and loyal members; government agencies; the residents of the six-county Scientific and Cultural Facilities District; and, of course, our visitors. Thanks to all of you for your support during our first 100 years. We look forward to serving you during the twenty-first century.

Enjoy exploring the Denver Museum of Nature and Science!

Raylene Decatur, President and C.E.O.

Information

Visiting the Museum

The Museum features incredible dioramas, priceless artifacts, and spectacular IMAX films.

The Basics

Here's all the essential information you'll need to know to plan your visit to the Museum.

Location The Museum is located at 2001 Colorado Boulevard in Denver, on the east end of City Park.

Parking Free parking is available in lots to the north and northwest of the main entrance. Accessible parking spaces can be found in these lots and to the east of the Museum.

Public transportation Several RTD routes stop outside the Museum on Colorado Boulevard. For route and schedule information, call RTD at 303-299-6000 or 1-800-366-RIDE.

Web site Visit www.dmns.org to get current information on hours, prices, exhibits, what's showing in the Phipps IMAX Theater, memberships, and other useful topics. You can also purchase advance tickets on the Web.

Hours The Museum is open daily except December 25, usually from 9:00 A.M. to 5:00 P.M. Check our Web site or call ahead for exact hours.

Cost There is an admission fee to the Museum. Reduced prices are available for children (ages 3–12), seniors (60+), and groups of twenty or more. Check our Web site or call for current prices.

Phipps IMAX Theater Films generally show on the hour. A separate admission fee is required. Combination Museum/IMAX tickets are available. Projected captions, amplification, and descriptive narrative are available for the hearing or sight impaired. Inquire at the box office at least twenty minutes prior to show time.

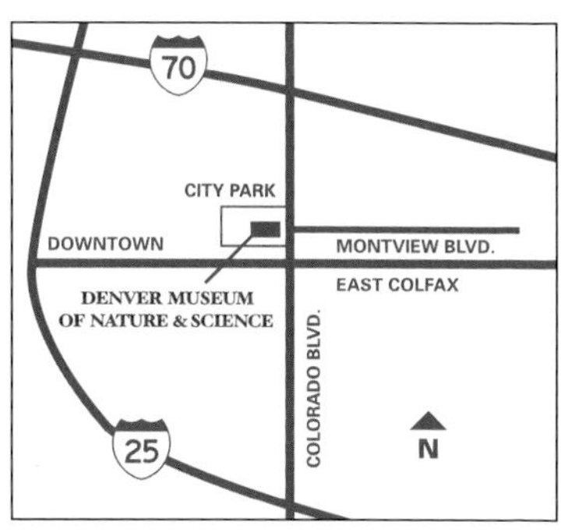

Call for Reservations and Information

303-322-7009 (Metro Denver)
1-800-925-2250 (Toll free)
303-370-8257 (TTY for hearing impaired)

Once You're Here

Food The T-Rex Cafe offers hot entrees, grilled sandwiches, pizza, salads, drinks, and desserts. The T-Rex Deli's menu includes made-to-order sandwiches, salads, drinks, pastries, and desserts. Both are open daily.

Museum Shop Features souvenirs, books, educational toys, clothing, and jewelry.

Information The friendly staff and volunteers at the Information desk will be happy to answer your questions. You can also call 303-370-6357.

Rest rooms Located throughout the Museum. Changing tables can be found in the rest rooms across from the escalators on all three floors.

Pay phones Located near the escalators on all three floors and by the main exit.

ATM Located by the Visitor and Member Services desk.

Stamps A vending machine is located by the Visitor and Member Services desk.

Mailbox Located outside the main exit.

Stroller, wheelchair, and cane rentals All can be checked out from the Information desk with a valid form of identification. Wheelchairs and canes are free. Strollers rent for $1.

Coin-operated lockers Available just inside the main entrance.

Taxicab service A courtesy phone at the Visitor and Member Services desk connects you directly with a taxicab dispatcher.

First aid Come to the Security post on the first floor near the main exit or ask any security guard for assistance.

Lost and found Come to the Security post on the first floor near the main exit.

For visitors with disabilities The Museum is accessible to physically challenged visitors. A brochure describing the services provided is available from the cashiers or at the Information desk.

Membership Free Museum admission, discounted IMAX tickets, and other benefits are available to Museum members. Call 303-370-6306, e-mail members@dmns.org, or stop by the Information desk for information or to purchase a membership.

The Inside Scoop

To help you decide what to see and do during your visit, we asked various Museum staff and visitors for their insiders' perspectives. Here's what they had to say.

Ten Tips for a Terrific Time

These helpful hints come from our Visitor Services staff—the people taking reservations, selling tickets, and checking in school groups. They'll do all they can to make your visit more enjoyable.

1. Give yourself plenty of time to tour the Museum and see an IMAX film.
2. Come on weekday afternoons or early in the morning on weekends when the Museum is often less crowded.
3. Make reservations in advance, especially to see an IMAX film on a weekend, over the Christmas holidays, or during spring break. Late afternoon is the best time to call for reservations.
4. Find out which temporary exhibitions, gallery programs, and other activities are being presented the day of your visit. Check our Web site or the information kiosks both outside and inside the Museum or ask at the Information desk.
5. Arrive early so you have time to park and pick up your tickets, especially if you have reservations for IMAX. You cannot enter the theater once the doors are closed.
6. Wear comfortable shoes and clothing.
7. Talk with the volunteers in the exhibit halls. They are there to answer your questions and to share touchable objects and fascinating activities.
8. Have lunch before 11:30 A.M. or after 1:00 P.M. to avoid lines at the T-Rex Cafe and Deli.
9. Arrange a place and time to meet in case your group gets separated. Some good meeting places: in front of the Museum Shop (first floor); by the moose on the second floor bridge; outside *Egyptian Mummies* (third floor).
10. Consider becoming a Museum member. Members get in free and can get discounted IMAX tickets at the Visitor and Member Services desk.

Visitors' Favorite Exhibits

- *Prehistoric Journey*
- *Edge of the Wild*
- Gems and Minerals
- North American Wildlife
- Bears and Sea Mammals

Alma King rhodochrosite crystal

Most Famous Objects

According to our curators, these ten objects are especially rare, valuable, or scientifically important.

- Folsom point *(Prehistoric Journey)*
- Alma King rhodochrosite crystal (Gems and Minerals)
- Tom's Baby gold nugget and Campion crystallized gold collection (Gems and Minerals)
- Reconstruction of Lucy *(Prehistoric Journey)*
- *Diplodocus (Prehistoric Journey)*
- Egyptian mummies
- William Clark's telescope
- Savuti Crossroads diorama *(Botswana: Safari to Wild Africa)*
- Passenger pigeons (Rare Birds)
- Maya Stela 3

Maya Stela 3, William Clark's telescope

NOTE: Because of construction for the space science exhibition, not all objects may be on display.

Kids' Top Five Favorite Things to See

- Hall of Life
- *Prehistoric Journey*
- IMAX
- *Egyptian Mummies*
- Gems and Minerals, Animal dioramas (tie)

Poor woman's mummy

More fun . . .

Fifteen permanent exhibitions and an IMAX theater can be just a starting point. While you're here, check out these other offerings.

Take in a Show

Stop by one of our gallery programs—short demonstrations on topics ranging from how animals walk to how to play African drums. Most shows involve audience participation. Schedules are posted throughout the Museum and are available at the ticket-taker booth.

Discovery Centers

Our discovery centers take a hands-on approach to exploring nature and science. Depending on the center's theme, you might get to dig up a fossil, handle a hissing cockroach, or make a sundial. Look for discovery centers during the summer and inside many of our temporary exhibitions.

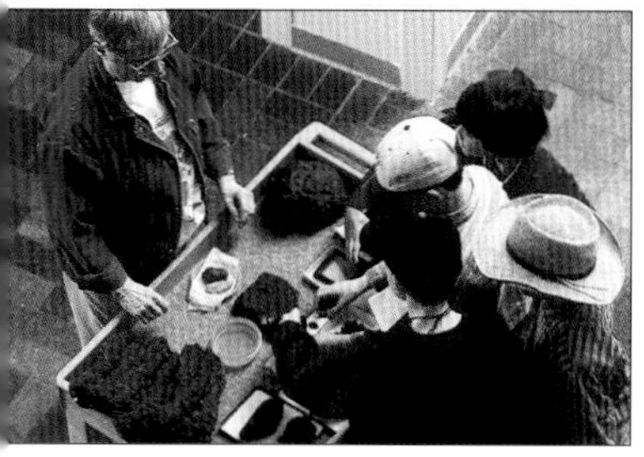

Please Touch

If you encounter a Museum volunteer standing next to a cart, stop! Here's your chance to touch real Museum objects. At our aptly named touch carts, you can hold a 150-million-year-old *Apatosaurus* tail, pet a bison, or study a human brain.

Elf Hunt

One of the artists who painted diorama backgrounds hid small elves in his works. Six are visible throughout the Museum. The elves are so well camouflaged, however, that they're almost impossible to find unless you know exactly where to look. Ask for the "Museum Seek-and-Find" sheet at the Information desk if you want to search for them.

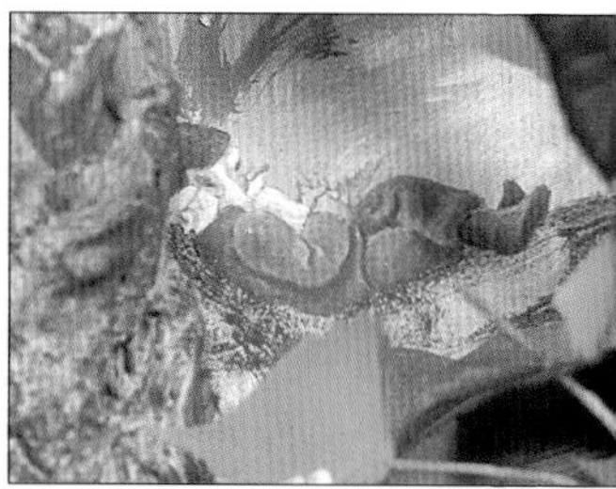

Our exhibits and collections include rare and fascinating objects. Among them are a life-size Tyrannosaurus rex *(inset), a Yup'ik mask (opposite, top), and a ceremonial Bering Sea Eskimo mask.*

Colorado Symbols Tour

Want to see most of Colorado's state symbols in an hour or two? Here's where you can find these official symbols of the Centennial State:

Flower • White and lavender columbine
Edge of the Wild and *Explore Colorado*

Bird • Lark bunting
Edge of the Wild and *Explore Colorado*

Insect • Colorado hairstreak butterfly
Insects

Grass • Blue grama
Edge of the Wild and *Explore Colorado*

Animal • Rocky Mountain bighorn sheep
Edge of the Wild

Tree • Colorado blue spruce
Explore Colorado

Gemstone • Aquamarine
Gems and Minerals

Fossil • *Stegosaurus*
Prehistoric Journey

Schoolchildren spearheaded the drive to name Stegosaurus *the state fossil.*

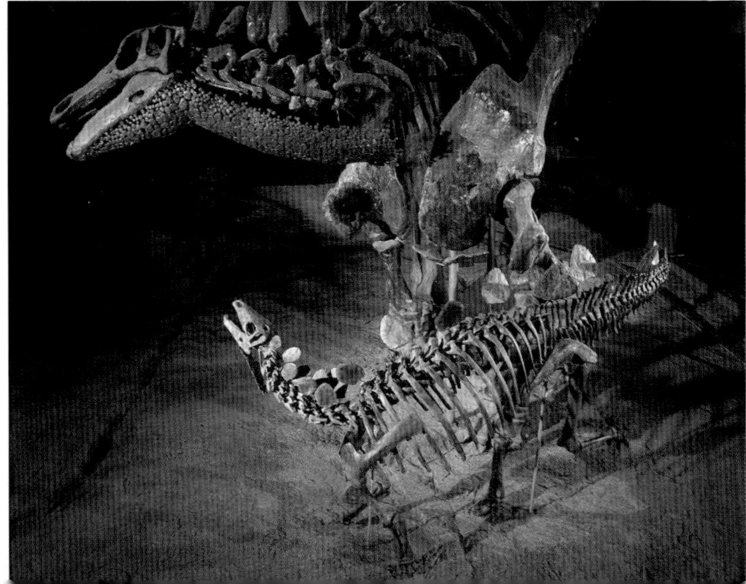

History

Exploring Our Past

Clockwise from above: H. Marie Wormington, our first curator of archaeology; Edwin Carter with our first collection, 1899; fieldwork, ca. 1927; assembling the Diplodocus, *ca. 1938*

A Brief History of the Museum

The Denver Museum of Nature and Science can trace its origins back more than a hundred years, to the efforts of one man in a little log cabin.

A New Museum for a New Century

In 1868, a pioneer naturalist named Edwin Carter arrived in Breckenridge, Colorado, and devoted himself to his true love: the scientific study of the birds and mammals of the Rocky Mountains. Almost single-handedly, Carter assembled one of the most complete collections of Colorado fauna in existence. He displayed his fine specimens in the Carter Museum, the log cabin that doubled as his home.

Word of Carter's collection spread around the state, and in 1892, a delegation of prominent Colorado citizens declared their interest in moving the collection to Denver for all to see. Considering Carter's advancing age, a museum in the state's capital seemed a fitting culmination of his efforts.

It took several years for the idea to become a reality. In 1897, Carter offered to sell his entire collection—valued by experts at between $30,000 and $50,000—for $10,000 to a group of Denver leaders intent on starting a museum. In return, he requested that a fireproof building be built and that he be appointed curator for life with a monthly salary of $150. John T. Mason and John F.

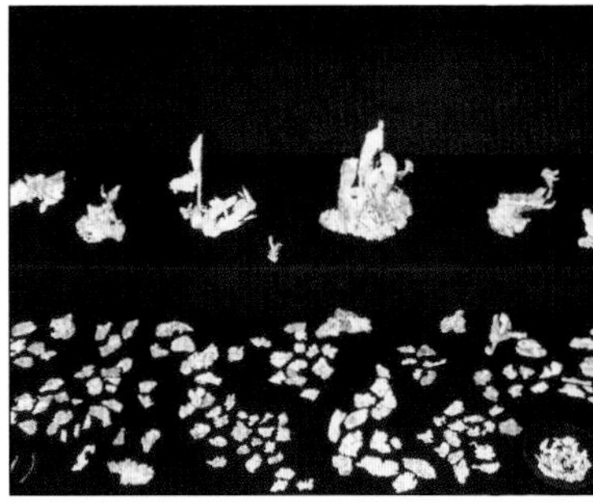

The Campion gold collection remains on display (above); key figures in our history (left, top to bottom): Edwin Carter, John T. Mason, John F. Campion.

The Carter Museum in Breckenridge, Colorado (left), provided the first specimens (right) for our zoology collections and exhibits.

Campion offered their impressive collections of butterflies and moths and crystalline gold, respectively, thereby providing the nucleus of a true natural history museum. In December 1899, with suitable funds in hand, the group finally accepted Carter's offer. Unfortunately, Carter never saw the realization of the dream. He died two months later, probably of arsenic poisoning, at the time an occupational hazard for taxidermists.

The Colorado Museum of Natural History was officially incorporated on December 6, 1900. In 1901, the new Board of Trustees hired the Museum's first staff members, a father-and-son team of taxidermists, to arrange and prepare Carter's collection. It had been moved to Denver by rail and was stored in the basement of the State Capitol. In October 1901, the Board and the City of Denver selected the site for the new museum—on the highest hill in City Park, with a spectacular, unobstructed view of the Rocky Mountains. Construction soon began on the Museum's first two buildings—the East Wing and the Central Wing *(opposite, top)*, completed in 1903 and 1908, respectively. The cost of the two wings totaled $107,933.64.

The Museum opened to the public on July 1, 1908. The Central Wing's three floors housed exhibits on birds, mammals, and rocks and minerals. About 12 percent of the Museum's 3,400 specimens were on display. Because of financial problems, the Museum almost did not survive its first year of public operation. Only repeated interventions by the mayor, asking the bank to allow overdrafts, kept the fledgling institution afloat.

The Museum's art gallery, 1908–1932

The first addition, 1918

Expanding Horizons

The Museum's situation improved significantly in 1910 with the hiring of its first professional director: Jesse D. Figgins, head of the Department of Preparation at the American Museum of Natural History in New York. Within a year, Figgins balanced the budget and established the range of activities—exhibition, education, fieldwork, and publication—that the Museum pursues to this day. By 1913, the Museum needed more space for its exhibits and collections. In those days, the City of Denver provided the lion's share of the Museum's operating budget, which averaged $27,000 a year, but the City couldn't afford $66,000 for an addition to the building's north end. Hopes for expansion dimmed during World War I, but then in 1917, Ellen M. Standley donated the necessary funds. Completed in 1918, the Joseph Standley Memorial Wing gave the staff three new exhibit halls to fill, complete with electric lighting.

Under Figgins, collecting and research efforts started with a biological survey of Colorado's birds and mammals and expanded from there. A crew headed to Florissant, Colorado, in 1915 on the Museum's first fossil-collecting expedition. In subsequent years, Figgins sent staff members farther afield to collect animal specimens for exhibits: Alaska (1921–1922); Paraguay, Brazil, and Argentina (1925–1926); Guyana and Brazil (1928); and Guatemala, Costa Rica, and Panama (1935–1936).

Fieldwork closer to home resulted in the most famous discovery ever made by Museum staff. In 1926, a crew working near Folsom, New Mexico, unearthed distinctive stone projectile points alongside the bones of an extinct bison species. These Folsom points revolutionized North American archaeology. At the time, scientists believed that humans had lived in North America

A taxidermist constructs a wood frame for a mounted moose.

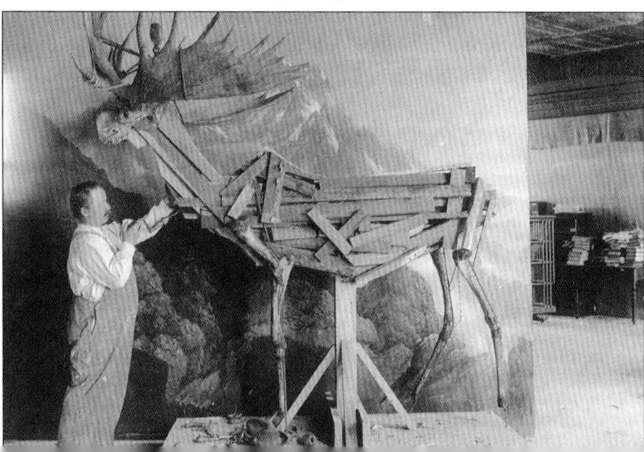

Folsom point amid an extinct bison's bones: Its discovery put the Museum on the map.

Removing fossils from the Folsom site, ca. 1927

for about 4,000 years. The Folsom point discovery placed people here thousands of years earlier, at the end of the last Ice Age, forcing the revision of theories about when the first humans arrived on this continent.

Not long after the return of the first South American expedition, construction began on a new South Wing in which to display the animals brought back. Donated by Elsie James Lemen and Harry C. James in memory of their father, the William H. James Memorial Wing opened to the public in 1929. At the same time, special programs for Denver schoolchildren and teachers took the Museum's collections to ever-widening audiences. Although the Museum hit rocky times with the Great Depression, by the time Figgins resigned in 1935, the institution was still in far better shape than it had been a quarter century earlier.

Establishing an International Reputation

In 1936 Alfred M. Bailey took the Museum's reins, and efforts to move the country out of the Great Depression began to have positive impacts on the institution. From 1936 through 1940, the federal Works Progress Administration (WPA) provided thirty-three to fifty additional employees to the Museum, more than doubling the size of the staff. The WPA workers rearranged and recataloged collections, chipped fossils out of rock, and made hundreds of thousands of "accessories," the fake plants used in exhibits. Their contributions

WPA workers making plants, 1938

A staff artist at work (left) on dinosaur murals that adorned our first floor from 1948 (above) to 1979

helped Bailey and his staff begin to create the large habitat dioramas seen today—with curved backgrounds, domed ceilings, tilted glass, and fluorescent lights.

During Bailey's long tenure, the Museum doubled in size. The first addition, dedicated in 1940, was a 950-seat auditorium, funded in part by Senator Lawrence C. Phipps. For the next forty years, Phipps Auditorium hosted hundreds of lectures, films, meetings, and concerts. A 1961 fire that started during a play rehearsal destroyed the building's interior, but an improved Phipps Auditorium opened seven months later.

Denver voters approved a $350,000 bond issue for construction of another addition in 1947. At the request of the mayor and the City Council, the institution changed its popular name in 1948 to the Denver Museum of Natural History, an acknowledgment of the city's long-standing support. Inflation and a steel shortage caused by the Korean War nearly doubled the price of the new West Wing and delayed its construction. When finally dedicated in 1953, the addition provided a new entrance, a scenic lounge, and lots more exhibit space.

Two new wings completed in 1968 provided even more room for growth. Spurred by a $1 million gift, the Southwest Wing, or Boettcher Foundation Wing, created space for the 235-seat Charles C. Gates Planetarium and planned halls of North American and African wildlife. The Northwest Wing paved the way for a small, 250-seat auditorium and areas for offices, collections, and exhibits, including the entire contents of the Southeast Museum of the North American Indian, donated by its owners, Francis V. and Mary W. A. Crane.

To fill the various additions, Museum staff journeyed to every continent except Antarctica to collect specimens and artifacts for exhibits. Destinations included Pacific Ocean islands; Australia; the museums of Europe; Canada; Mexico; subantarctic Campbell

Director Bailey making friends with the natives, Australia, 1949

Island; the Galápagos Islands; Botswana, Africa; and Alaska. Bailey personally led several of these expeditions. He also oversaw numerous expansions in educational programming, ranging from the addition of a Denver Public Schools teacher to the staff in 1954 to the creation of a Department of Education in 1969. By the time Bailey retired in 1969, the Museum was known around the world for its programs, fieldwork, and wildlife dioramas.

An Ever-Evolving Museum

Since 1970, four directors—Roy E. Coy, Charles T. Crockett, John G. Welles, and Raylene Decatur—have guided the Museum through times of tremendous growth and change. During the 1970s and 1980s, the Museum unveiled exhibits of North American, South American, and African wildlife; a gem and mineral hall; and the new Crane American Indian Hall, the first containing dioramas depicting human cultures. Temporary exhibitions became a regular attraction, with subjects ranging from Southeast Asian textiles to robotic dinosaurs. Gates Planetarium was renovated and outfitted with a new star projector, and Phipps Auditorium was transformed into the world's twelfth IMAX theater. Educational programs continued to expand, offering more and more learning opportunities for people from 3 to 93, both inside the Museum and out in the field.

Starting in 1972, people could purchase a Museum membership. Members could attend new Saturday workshops or travel with staff to faraway lands. They also helped bolster an institution

Solar eclipse expedition, Kenya, 1973

that was increasingly in need of funding as support from the City of Denver ebbed in the early 1980s.

The eventual loss of government funding forced the Museum to begin charging admission in 1982. That same year, Denver voters overwhelmingly passed a $20 million bond issue to modernize the Museum's aging facilities and to expand the building eastward. The original 1903 building was demolished in 1985 to make room for fifty-foot-high atria that would connect two new wings to the Museum. Completed in 1987, the additions moved the main entrance to the north side of the building and contained a new shop and cafeteria. The new additions also provided classroom and exhibit space for the Hall of Life, which merged with the Museum in 1985; ample room for the blockbuster exhibitions *Ramses II: The Great Pharaoh and His Time, AZTEC: The World of Moctezuma,* and *Imperial Tombs of China;* a spot for a glassed-in fossil preparation lab; and a home for the Museum's exhibition chronicling life on Earth, which opened in 1995.

In 1988, voters in the metro area approved the creation of the Scientific and Cultural Facilities District (SCFD)—a 0.1 percent sales tax that supports institutions like the Museum. Denver and the surrounding counties pioneered this method of supporting their cultural and educational organizations. SCFD funds provided long-term financial stability and allowed the Museum to bring more traveling exhibitions to town and renovate old diorama halls. Behind the scenes, staff used some of these moneys to ensure that the 650,000 objects in the collections will be preserved for another hundred years and beyond. The Museum was also able to place more emphasis on scientific research. Out in the field, Museum scientists studied wildlife populations in Colorado; excavated plant and animal fossils throughout the region; and searched for signs of ancient humans in coastal Alaskan caves.

Gates Planetarium control panel, star machine, and dome, 1982–2000

The most recent additions under construction, 1985

Clockwise from above: Popular temporary exhibitions have included AZTEC, Cruisin' the Fossil Freeway, *and* Imperial Tombs of China.

Summer finds our staff and volunteers out in the field, trapping mammals (left) and excavating fossils (above).

As the Museum approached its centennial celebration in 2000, it changed its name to more accurately reflect its mission and to emphasize the importance of nature and science for the twenty-first century. From its first day, the newly christened Denver Museum of Nature and Science claimed an annual visitation of more than 1.5 million, a staff of 500, an operating budget in excess of $20 million a year, and the largest volunteer corps of any natural history museum in the country.

In 1894, Edwin Carter wrote, "As Denver is destined to be among the great Cities of the Continent, so will a museum here founded . . . grow up to be one of the great entertaining and educational institutions of the country." The events of the intervening century seem to have proven Carter right.

Come on in! Tyrannosaurus rex *greets visitors at the main entrance.*

Exhibits

Floor 1

Clockwise from top: Alma King rhodochrosite; morpho butterfly; Insects exhibit; the Orion Nebula as seen from the Hubble Space Telescope

Gems and Minerals

Coors Mineral Hall

Dig into sparkling displays of minerals, precious gemstones, and Colorado's mining heritage.

Gems and Minerals features the best of the Museum's geology collections. Specimen-packed display cases show off minerals from around the world, glittering gems, and the valuable minerals that have played a starring role in Colorado's history.

Minerals of the World

The crown jewel of Coors Mineral Hall is the Alma King, the largest and finest known rhodochrosite crystal on Earth. Embedded in a delicate matrix of white quartz and purple fluorite crystals, the five-by-seven-inch (14-by-17-cm), cherry red crystal was discovered on August 21, 1992, in the Sweet Home Mine, near the tiny hamlet of Alma, Colorado. By sheer luck, a Museum video crew accompanied the miners that fateful

Mexican miners in the early 1900s hold crystals like those in our crystal cavern (right).

"Bosom Pals," one of Vasily Konovalenko's popular gem carvings; chunks of pyrite, turquoise, and copper (below, from top)

day. You can witness the historic discovery for yourself on the monitors flanking this Colorado treasure.

Another of the hall's highlights—a crystal treasure from Mexico—has been enjoyed by generations of visitors. This reconstructed cavern features specimens collected deep in silver mines in northern Mexico. In the center and to the right are calcite and aragonite formations first installed in the Museum in 1912. Large gypsum crystals cover the cavern's left wall. Museum staff collected them in the 1960s, carefully chipping 250-pound (113-kg) slabs of crystals off the mine's walls in sweltering, 100-degree (38°C) heat. The reconstructed cavern debuted in 1975.

Two years after unearthing the Alma King, Sweet Home miners discovered a large pocket of exquisite rhodochrosites. The mine's owner suggested re-creating the pocket inside the Museum to show how the crystals formed. Thirty million years ago, hot mineral-rich waters seeped up into cracks in the rock. As the waters cooled, manganese carbonate minerals precipitated out onto the granite walls, forming rhodochrosite crystals. Crews used hydraulic splitters, diamond chain saws, and chisels to extract the crystals from the mine piece by piece. It took six months to clean and a year to reassemble the thousands of fragile pieces. The resulting seven-by-eight-foot (2.1-by-2.4-m) wall, installed in a simulated mine tunnel in 1997, gives you the chance to explore the rhodochrosites' original home.

Outside the mine, hands-on exhibits provide a crash course in how to recognize minerals based on their physical properties. Then you proceed through a mineral lover's mecca. Twenty-three

"Inside" the Sweet Home Mine

cases containing more than 650 specimens display the incredible variety of colors, shapes, sizes, and textures in which minerals come: bright yellow sulfur crystals, shiny cubes of pyrite, deep blue chunks of azurite, orangish crystals of wulfenite. In the process, you can see the world—small pieces of it, that is. Specimens hail from such far-flung locales as Norway, Tasmania, and Madagascar. Among the specimens you encounter as you wend your way through the hall are the economically important metallic ores, the very common silicates (which make up 90 percent of the rocks in Earth's crust), and an amethyst quartz geode weighing more than 500 pounds (230 kg).

Gems

A small darkened room showcases our collection of precious gems. Unlike most of our other collections, almost all of our gems are displayed here. The highlight is a 10,588-carat topaz from Brazil *(above)*. One of the largest faceted stones in the world, it was once owned by Salvador Dali, the Spanish surrealist. Dali intended to have people view a nude Venus painted inside a gold cup through the topaz. The only problem: It was impossible to see the painting through the stone's 129 facets.

The gem exhibit also houses collections of opals, sapphires, and other treasures from around the world, and glass models of famous diamonds. Two cases of Colorado gems feature the stones in both their rough and cut forms.

Colorado Minerals and Mining

Mining for everything from gold to molybdenite has been an important part of Colorado's history. The third section of Gems and Minerals focuses on the state's most valuable minerals.

The exhibit's centerpiece is the gold and silver room, home of the John F. Campion collection of crystallized gold from Breckenridge, Colorado. Campion, the Museum's first president, offered his collection in 1899 to help start the institution. These beautiful gold pieces

A Colorado miner, ca. 1875–1890

B-I-N-G-O! Excited miners marvel at their newfound treasure: the Alma King, the world's largest rhodochrosite crystal. It now resides in its quartz-and-fluorite matrix in Coors Mineral Hall.

Tom's Baby: Discovered twice

have been on display since 1909—longer than any other objects in the Museum. The gold was originally embedded in soft rock, but Campion had the rock dissolved with acid, leaving the glittering crystallized gold you see today.

Also located in the gold and silver room is Tom's Baby, the largest single mass of crystallized gold ever found in Colorado. Two miners discovered this spectacular nugget in Breckenridge in 1887. (It got its name from the way one of them cradled it affectionately.) It was rediscovered—in pieces in a downtown Denver bank vault—by Museum staff in 1972. Donated as part of the Campion gold collection, Tom's Baby had apparently been placed in a safe-deposit box in 1929 and forgotten! Two pieces fit back together to create the eight-and-a-half-pound (3.9-kg) specimen now on display. A third piece found in the bank vault may be part of Tom's Baby (which originally weighed eleven pounds [5 kg]), but this nugget doesn't fit with the other two. The "missing" piece remains a mystery.

Other highlights in this part of Coors Mineral Hall include the Gold Boulder of Summitville, discovered in 1975 along a mining road; a diorama showing a cavity of amazonite and smoky quartz crystals where it was found near Pikes Peak; and a small case of aquamarine, Colorado's state gemstone. The final alcove displays minerals from the state's mining districts—from the Front Range to central Colorado to the San Juan Mountains. Historic photographs reveal old mining techniques, among them transporting men and material via aerial tramway, the predecessor of the modern ski lift.

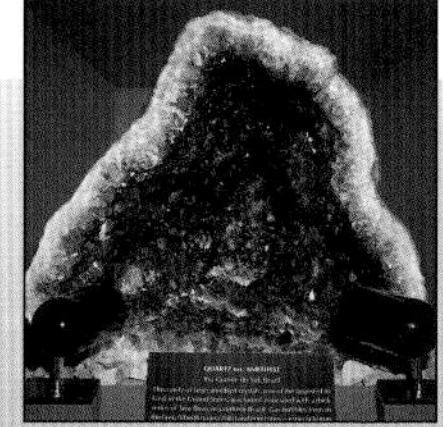

- Staff nicknamed the huge amethyst quartz geode *(right)* "Jaws," after the famous shark movie.
- A cleverly placed mirror makes the Mexican crystal cavern appear larger than it really is.
- The Gold Boulder of Summitville contains more gold than the amount that started the Pikes Peak gold rush in 1859.
- William Coors christened Coors Mineral Hall in 1982 by smashing a bottle of his company's beer over a large mineral.

Insects

Take a few minutes to meet the world's largest group of animals.

This small exhibit provides a brief look at insects, including beautiful butterflies and moths. Insects may be relatively small in size, but their numbers are huge. Insects account for three out of every four animal species. That translates to more than 760,000 known insect species.

The exhibit's first two sections examine what insects are, how scientists classify them, and how insects survive in a "bird-eat-bug" world. Some advertise their unpalatability; others blend in with their surroundings, as you can (or can't) see in the small diorama. The Colorado Lepidoptera section displays 171 different species of butterflies and moths, including the Colorado hairstreak butterfly, the official state insect. The fourth section of the exhibit illustrates the life cycle of a butterfly—from egg to larva (caterpillar) to pupa (cocoon) to adult—with larger-than-life models.

Finding the twenty-one insects in this case is a real challenge.

Completed in 1990, Insects moved from the second floor to this spot in 1993. With the exception of the diorama, the specimens here look exactly like they do in our collections—lots and lots of pinned bugs, beetles, and butterflies.

Space Science Exhibition

Coming soon: Your chance to explore the universe and our place in it.

Ever wondered what it would be like to see Earth from orbit? To visit another planet? To travel across the universe? When the Museum opens its new, multimillion-dollar space science exhibition in 2003, you'll be able to have these experiences without ever leaving the ground.

Our space science project represents a dynamic new addition to the Museum—one that will offer experiences you won't find anywhere else. You'll get a sense of what it's like to be in space. You'll make your own personal discoveries about our universe, and you'll find that space technology may affect your life more than you imagined. You and your family and friends will have lots to talk about as you ponder the origins of the universe, Earth's place in it, the human relationship to the sky, and whether life exists beyond Earth. (Amazingly, some space scientists think we'll be able to answer this age-old question within the next fifty years.)

Much of your experience will be based on the concept of going on a trip. Half the fun of traveling is anticipating and preparing for the journey. You might start your trip to outer space at a visitor center to the universe, where a galactic travel agent will help you plan your trip. Like any good travel agent, they'll help you sort through the available destinations and select the ones that are right for you. Perhaps you'll also want to research some possible destinations in our resource center, which will be linked to the Museum's new digital collection of images and information about space. Before departing, you can visit our astronaut

Get so close to planets you'll almost be able to touch them.

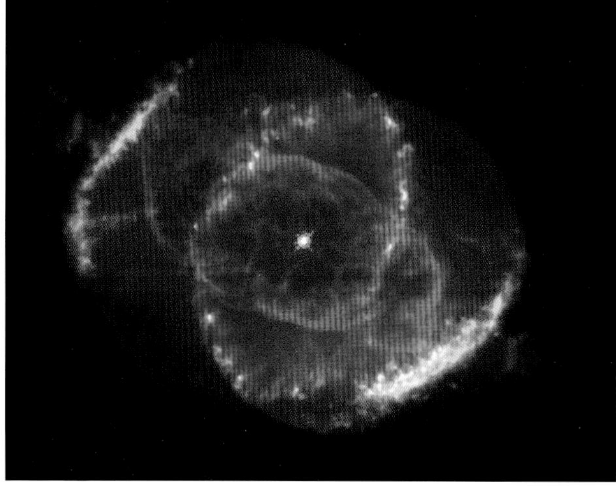

Explore the Cat's Eye Nebula using our digital collection; Earth (below).

training center. Try on a space suit, experiment with the tools and instruments used by astronauts, and maybe even feel what it's like to walk in a low-gravity environment like the Moon's. You'll come to appreciate the challenges of working and living in a place with no oxygen, extreme temperatures, and lots of radiation.

Destination: Space

Having prepared for your space adventure, you'll embark for any or all of three destinations, each one farther and farther from Earth. You can start in low Earth orbit aboard a space station. Outside the windows, spinning slowly beneath you, will be our home planet—a fragile blue marble in the blackness of space. (Well, a large digital representation of this awesome sight.) Aboard the station, you'll study our planet just as astronauts and other Earth researchers do. Monitor real-time weather systems, or examine the impacts of natural events, such as volcanic eruptions, or human-caused changes, such as deforestation. Use data from satellites to zoom in on and explore the geography and geology of the Front Range. You'll leave orbit with a whole new appreciation for the fragility and beauty of our home.

A second destination will be a planet outpost. From inside this research base, you'll look out panoramic windows onto another world: the rocky red surface of Mars, the gray craters of the Moon, Venus, or even an asteroid. With this exhibit, the Museum plans to take dioramas into the twenty-first century. The background of this planetary scene won't be painted; instead it will be a huge video screen. Perhaps dust devils will swirl past in the distance as the Sun sweeps realistically across the sky. The foreground (the planet's surface) will be simulated as realistically as possible and will also serve as a stage. A robotic rover might roam the surface collecting rock samples, or maybe you'll see and talk to an astronaut conducting experiments outside the base. Earth will seem especially inviting once you've compared it to living on another planet.

Deep space could be your third destination. In a small theater in which time and the laws of physics are suspended, you'll travel to places seen only with advanced telescopes. Through the magic of supercomputers, incredibly detailed maps of the universe, and digital projection systems, you'll visit nebulae, black holes, new stars, and exploding stars. You'll be able to travel back in time to the cosmic origins of our universe, and you'll return home with a new awareness of its immensity, complexity, and beauty.

Gates Planetarium and Celebrating the Sun

Another major component of the space science exhibition will be a completely renovated Gates Planetarium. Its dome will be enlarged slightly and tilted, and its 140 seats will face in one direction and will be placed on a slope. Advanced computer graphics and video systems and the latest sound and light effects will create magnificent night skies and journeys to other times and places. This spectacular technology will be teamed with live performers, demonstrations, and audience participation.

The new facility will be a far cry from our first planetarium, which opened in 1955 with eighty seats under a twenty-foot (6-m) metal fabric dome on the third floor. The theater moved to its current location and became the 235-seat Charles C. Gates Planetarium in 1968. Between 1968 and 2000, two different star projectors and numerous computer control and video projection systems illuminated the fifty-foot (15-m) dome, educating and entertaining millions of visitors.

Surrounding the Planetarium will be a discovery center celebrating our nearest star, the Sun. New windows will let Colorado's abundant sunshine inside, and amid the tents and booths in a festival-like setting, you'll find activities and scientific instruments you can use to study the Sun for yourself. Observe

First planetarium, 1955; Mars (top)

Thanks to the Hubble Space Telescope, we can now observe galaxies billions of light-years away and planetary nebulae, such as the Twin Jet Nebula (inset).

Gallery programs (insets) will be a crucial component of our new space science exhibition; the Eagle Nebula, where stars form inside giant pillars of gas.

real-time solar flares or sunspots with a filtered telescope, or show a youngster how a prism breaks white sunlight into a spectrum of colors. You'll finally get to look at the Sun without hurting your eyes.

Tip of the Asteroid

The 38,000 square feet (3,530 sq m) of experience-based exhibits and programming represent just the "tip of the asteroid" of our space science project. Behind the scenes will be new staff, collections, and programs to support our renewed commitment to space science education. Our scientists have begun collecting digital, space-related images and data to provide content and illustrations for exhibits and programs. Partnerships with NASA and local space-related companies and research institutions will allow us to make full use of one another's resources and opportunities. We will also be expanding both on- and off-site educational programs in an effort to build a stronger, more scientifically literate community.

Whether you visit in 2003 or 2008, our space science exhibits and programs will be new and up-to-date. Their design and extensive use of digital technology will allow Museum staff to respond quickly to astronomical events and research. With new discoveries being announced almost weekly, human knowledge of space is growing at an unprecedented rate. Our space science exhibition promises to provide an exciting environment in which you can brush up on the latest revelations, ponder our ever-evolving place in the universe, and experience space for yourself.

Experiment with the Sun and a beach ball to understand seasons; Saturn (above).

See the Sun in a whole new light with the help of Museum astronomers.

fun facts

- On Christmas Eve 1968, Planetarium staff used a twenty-two-inch (56-cm) telescope with a television camera attached to try to see the Apollo 8 spacecraft circling the Moon. NBC broadcast their pictures to a television audience estimated at 70 million.
- The star machine used from 1982 to 2000 could project 4,326 stars onto the dome simultaneously.
- Over the years, such luminaries as Isaac Asimov and Leonard Nimoy have written or narrated our Planetarium's productions.

Exhibits

Floor 2

Clockwise from top: Colorado grizzlies; Sioux beaded vest; "dining out" in the Hall of Life; raccoon; koalas from Australia

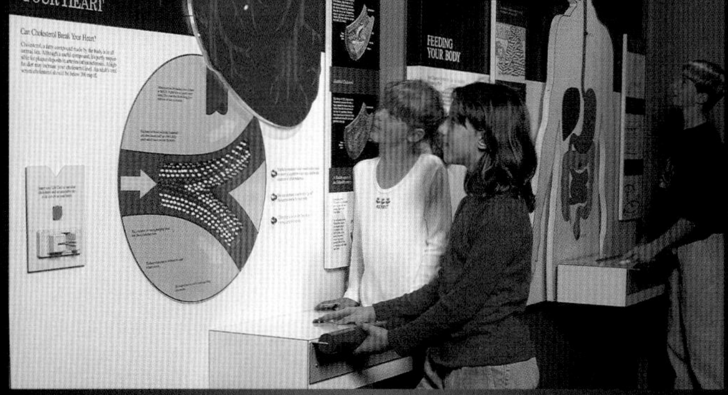

Hall of Life

Have more fun than you could imagine learning how your body works and how to keep it working well.

The Hall of Life sets the DMNS apart from most other natural history museums by offering our visitors engaging health science exhibits. The Museum's first completely interactive exhibition, the Hall of Life consistently ranks as one of our most popular offerings.

The LifeCard you receive at the Hall's entrance is your key to the exhibition. The LifeCard activates exhibits and, at certain stations, records information to create a personal health profile you can print out at the Hall's exit.

How Your Body Works

The Hall of Life looks first at the human body. After a brief introduction, a series of exhibits traces the wondrous process of human development—from a single cell smaller than a period on this page to a fully formed baby in thirty-eight weeks. Featured in several places are the works of Lennart Nilsson, the renowned biological photographer who captured amazing images inside women's wombs. This section also provides the rare opportunity to see actual embryos and fetuses. The twelve specimens—obtained in the 1950s and sadly all the result of pregnancies ended by accident, illness, or stillbirth—were donated to the Museum by the American Medical Association through the University of Illinois School of Medicine.

Stretch your body and your mind.

A great way to answer that "Where do babies come from?" question

Across from the human development section are life-size models that provide an inside look at human anatomy. The human body is an incredibly complex organism made up of billions of cells. The exhibits just highlight the major bones, organs, and types of joints. Around the corner, exhibits on genetics show how genes, the basic units of heredity, affect everything from your appearance to your health. The last section on the human body deals with the five senses. Here you can learn the simple mechanics of how our eyes, ears, nose, tongue, and skin help us perceive the world.

Healthy Choices

The rest of the Hall of Life focuses on how we treat our bodies. Each day we make dozens of decisions about our health—what to eat; whether to exercise; how to deal with stress; whether to smoke, drink, or take drugs. "Choices" gives you the chance to assess your current health habits and find out how you could improve upon them.

After the computerized check-in station, the first section explores nutrition. Various exhibits provide tips on eating a healthy diet and the fat, cholesterol, and sodium content of various foods. You can also "visit" Chinese, Mexican, and Italian restaurants (via interactive videos) to see how your favorites stack up nutritionally.

The fitness section touts the numerous benefits of an exercise program. Here you can take your pulse and blood pressure, measure your flexibility, and test your

How high can you jump?

Step up to a healthier lifestyle.

cardiovascular fitness. Bet you never expected to leave a museum exhibit huffing and puffing! You can also figure out what type of exercise might be best for you.

Feeling stressed out? Discover how stress affects your body in the next section. Take a computer quiz to analyze your current stress level, and then spend a few minutes practicing relaxation techniques.

The final section examines the impacts of drugs on the body. Preserved human lungs reveal the effects of smoking, and other exhibits detail the physical consequences of taking narcotics. The popular drunk-driving simulators show you just how impaired your reaction time is after a few drinks.

Devoting some time to the Hall of Life is a great step toward a healthier lifestyle. It's also a lot more fun than a visit to the doctor!

How the Hall of Life Was Born

The Hall of Life began its existence as a separate institution founded by a local physician. In 1975, Dr. Leo Nolan and a group of medical and educational leaders persuaded Blue Cross Blue Shield of Colorado to donate office and exhibit space in its building at 7th and Broadway in Denver. Health education classes began there in 1979. To reach a larger audience, the Hall of Life merged with the Museum and moved into its current space in 1987. When the final phase of exhibits opened in 1990, the Hall of Life became one of the largest hands-on health education centers in North America.

That's one! And two! And step! The cardiovascular fitness test

Sure you want those chips? Measure your health-smart shopping skills at the Eat-Rite Supermarket exhibit.

fun facts

- The Hall of Life serves more than 100,000 people each year through its statewide outreach programs.
- Colorado schoolchildren create antismoking posters for a national contest called Tar Wars, which started at the Hall of Life in 1988.
- The Hall of Life's interactive restaurant exhibits have served more than 2 million meals since their debut in 1990.

Bears and Sea Mammals

Ella M. Dalton Hall

Walk right up to polar bears, grizzlies, and walruses—and live to tell about it!

Bears and sea mammals are impressive, powerful animals. The ten dioramas in Dalton Hall allow you to see just how magnificent they are. Featured in re-creations of their natural habitats are polar bears; huge Alaskan brown bears; black bears, including rare white and glacier-blue color phases; grizzlies; several species of seals; two species of sea lions; and walruses *(above)*. The sites depicted range from Colorado to California and up the coast to British Columbia and Alaska. Many visitors appreciate the (usually) quiet, contemplative atmosphere of this hall. It's a great place simply to enjoy the dioramas.

Scientists classify all the hall's featured animals as mammals (animals that have hair and feed their young milk from the mother). In fact, bears, seals, sea lions, and walruses belong to the same order, or group, of mammals: the Carnivora, or carnivores. Scientists consider them carnivores not because of what they eat but because they all have sharp teeth adapted to tearing and shearing flesh. They all evolved from a common ancestor that lived about 40 million years ago.

Museum dogsled team in Alaska, 1922

Eight of the dioramas show adult males and females, perhaps with youngsters. This format gives visitors the chance to see any differences between the sexes, which are most obvious in the walruses. You also get to see some incredibly cute cubs. Such scenes, however, are not always completely accurate. For example, a female polar bear would almost never allow a male to get this close to her two cubs. He could easily consider the cubs prey.

Native hunters hauling a bearded seal, 1922

Historic Specimens

Although most of Dalton Hall's dioramas were constructed during World War II, three contain specimens collected decades earlier. In 1921, the Museum sent two men, including future director Alfred M. Bailey, on a sixteen-month expedition to Alaska. Traveling by U.S. Coast Guard cutter and dogsled, our two staff members hunted or purchased the specimens now displayed in the walrus, polar bear, glacier-blue black bear, and Canadian grizzly dioramas.

To obtain the walruses, Bailey joined Eskimo hunters in open skin boats called umiaks. They sailed and paddled among ice floes for up to two days at a stretch as the walruses migrated through the Bering Strait separating Alaska and Siberia. The animals they killed provided food for the local residents. Only when they could safely add a heavy, thick walrus skin to a load of meat did Bailey

This black bear diorama depicts the bears in Yellowstone National Park.

Bears and more bears (from top): white black bears known as Kermodes bears; an Alaskan brown bear; grizzlies in Colorado; polar bears

get a specimen for the Museum. Thanks to stormy weather that scuttled numerous hunts, it took Bailey and the hunters nearly two months to secure enough walruses for their winter meals and our diorama.

How the male polar bear wound up in a diorama also makes an interesting story. In March 1922, a sixteen-year-old Eskimo girl and her intended husband heard their sled dogs barking furiously outside her parents' sod igloo. Peeking out through the top, they discovered the bear raiding their cache of frozen seals. According to Bailey's journal, they both "pumped lead until the old 'nannuk' was fit for a scientific specimen." Knowing of Bailey's collecting efforts, the young couple took the skin with them to the village of Wainwright, where the schoolteacher was to marry them. Bailey paid the couple $55 for the fine specimen—a nice start to their honeymoon.

Four other dioramas in the Museum feature specimens from that 1921–1922 expedition. They include the caribou in North American Wildlife's Bonfils Hall and several avian species in three dioramas in Rare Birds.

fun facts

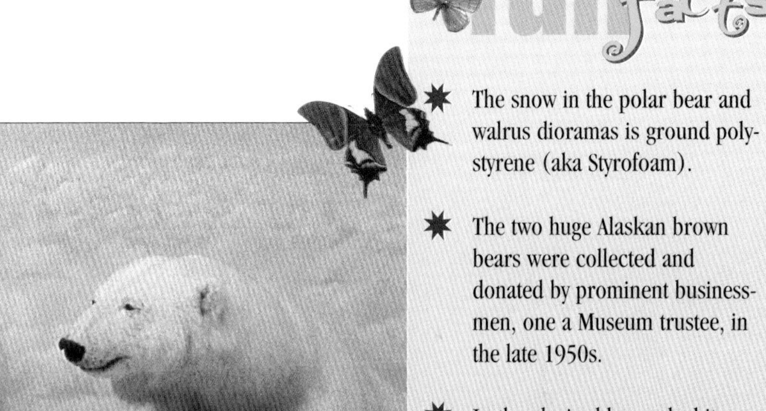

- The snow in the polar bear and walrus dioramas is ground polystyrene (aka Styrofoam).
- The two huge Alaskan brown bears were collected and donated by prominent businessmen, one a Museum trustee, in the late 1950s.
- In the glacier-blue and white black bear dioramas, a hidden mirror reflects light up to illuminate a bear's face.
- The skin, skeleton, and skull of Colorado's last known grizzly bear reside in our zoology collections. The bear died in 1979.

Edge of the Wild

Charles Boettcher Colorado Hall

Come face-to-face with Colorado's famous wildlife.

Edge of the Wild introduces you to Coloradans' wild animal neighbors. Eight stunning dioramas depict the state's large mammals in their natural habitats. You can see mountain lions, bighorn sheep, mule deer, white-tailed deer, elk, bison, and pronghorn, getting closer than you'd ever want to be in the wild.

The exhibition presents the animals' natural history—what they eat, how they get their food, how they raise their families, where they live, and how their bodies are adapted to help them survive. Another key theme is their contact and conflict with humans during the past 100 years. Back when the wild game herds seemed endless, people killed these animals by the thousands or even millions. Now we carefully manage their remaining populations, which is the only hope they have of surviving as human populations grow and cities expand. The exhibit notes, "When you see wild animals in your backyard, chances are it's because you've moved into theirs."

Each diorama captures a moment in time in the lives of the animals. A female mountain lion brings her three kittens to a freshly killed and cached mule deer in Colorado National Monument. A herd of mule deer migrates to lower elevations west of Colorado Springs as a winter storm approaches. Near Mount Evans, a bull elk bugles to attract a mate while an unsuspecting calf investigates a porcupine. A male bison rolls in the dust to scratch his back; another just loafs on a midwinter day in South Park. Museum staff selected a specific site in Colorado for each diorama and made detailed studies of the plant and animal life there. This fieldwork ensured that both the foregrounds and the painted backgrounds would be as realistic as possible.

Edge of the Wild offers you the chance to explore with (almost) all of your senses. Look for the small animals and

Yes, it's real: a mule deer buck in a lush montane forest south of Vail.

wildflowers tucked into the foregrounds. Listen to an elk bugling, or hear a description of a diorama through the telephone handset at the diorama's side. Smell the scent produced by a mule deer's glands. Touch bison fur or a mountain lion skull. Many of these innovations were originally developed to make the exhibition more accessible to people with disabilities. The end result is a hall that is more enjoyable for everyone.

Evolution of a Hall

Boettcher Hall has housed exhibits about mammals for more than ninety years. At first the animals were displayed in simple cases in traditional statuesque "trophy" poses. In the early 1930s, the Museum's small staff enlarged the exhibits, placed the animals in more naturalistic settings, and devoted the hall exclusively to large Colorado mammals. Extensive renovations from 1948 to 1955 created the existing diorama shells with fifty-foot-wide (15-m), curved backgrounds. Museum staff chose the sites still depicted today. The pronghorn and white-tailed deer dioramas were substantially revised in the early 1980s, but three others look much like they did fifty years ago—with a bit of sprucing up.

The current exhibition resulted from a major renovation in the early 1990s. Funded by the Scientific and Cultural Facilities District, the twenty-nine-month, $810,000 project involved adding new interpretive panels and interactive exhibits and thoroughly cleaning the dioramas. Over the years the flowers had faded,

Please touch! A bighorn's horn

1913

1933

1955

leaves had curled, and the animal specimens had accumulated dust. Museum staff carefully vacuumed each animal. The plants took a bit more work. Two dozen volunteers helped staff replace, restore, or straighten every leaf and blade of grass in several dioramas. Many new birds and reptiles and more than a dozen species of insects were added to increase the realism of the scenes.

Three dioramas—bison, mountain lion, and elk—received substantial makeovers. Museum taxidermists worked with curators to show the new animals in more active, scientifically accurate poses. For example, the two male bison replaced a family group. Research into bison behavior indicated that mature males, females, and calves do not herd together in midwinter, the season depicted in the diorama. A male mountain lion was removed because males are solitary except during the mating season; they do not participate in raising the young. One other significant change was placing an ear tag on one of the bighorn sheep. The simple addition vividly illustrates the hall's theme of human interactions with wildlife.

The evolution of our mountain lion diorama, from 1913 (top) to the present (below)

fun facts

- In the summer mule deer diorama *(above)*, some of the aspen trees have fluorescent lights embedded in their trunks to light the background.
- *Edge of the Wild* received the American Association of Museums 1996 Accessibility Award for its thoughtful design and participatory, hands-on exhibitry.
- The farm painted in the background of the white-tailed deer diorama represents the first sign of humans changing the environment in one of our ecological dioramas. The farm was added by a staff artist in 1981.

North American Wildlife

Boettcher North American Hall and Frederick G. Bonfils Hall

Discover the diversity of North America's magnificent wild creatures.

North American Wildlife presents our continent's wonderful variety of wild animals and the places they inhabit. Nineteen spectacular dioramas depict scenes ranging from the frigid mountains of Alaska to the dry grasslands of Colorado to the warm waters of a Florida river. In most cases, the dioramas' centerpieces are mammals. They include numerous species of hoofed mammals in addition to well-known canines, felines, and mustelids (weasel relatives). Rarely will you see so many different racks of antlers, massive horns, and gorgeous coats of fur all in one place.

Two distinct halls make up North American Wildlife. The rectangular Bonfils Hall was completed in 1971. Its ten dioramas focus mostly on big game and fur-bearing animals of the Far North—Alaska, British Columbia, Ellesmere Island (west of northern Greenland). Colorado and Wyoming locales round out the ten sites. The featured animals include wolverines *(top),* Stone sheep, Canada lynx, a pine marten, mountain goats, wolves, Dall sheep, musk oxen, caribou, and mink. All of these animals possess thick winter coats (and other adaptations) that insulate them from the arctic chill.

The other half of North American Wildlife is Boettcher North American Hall, the circular one of the two halls, which was completed in 1982. Six of its dioramas depict Colorado's beavers, coyotes, and Mexican free-tailed bats; Alaska's moose, caribou, and Sitka black-tailed deer; and Florida's manatees. The other dioramas focus more on habitats than wildlife, contrasting the deciduous forests of Tennessee's Great Smoky Mountains with the dense temperate rainforests of Washington State. You have to look a bit harder to find the mammals in these dioramas.

Several cases display American Indian artifacts related to North American wildlife. Clothing and food containers made from hides and horns illustrate the Indians' historical dependence on animals for life's necessities. Ceremonial objects depicting animals speak to the reverence Native Americans have traditionally shown for their four-legged brothers.

Artifacts made from animal hides

Endangered Species, Cultures, and Sites

Three dioramas in North American Wildlife highlight species in trouble: the West Indian manatee, the Canada lynx, and the wolf. The gentle, aquatic manatee has been considered an endangered species by the federal government since 1967. When Museum staff conducted fieldwork in Florida in 1980, they had no intention of collecting a manatee. Instead they used measurements and molds from other sources to create life-size sculptures. The female manatee and her calf are fiberglass models made from those sculptures, not real taxidermy mounts. The diorama helps make people aware of the plight of the remaining manatee population.

Swimming with manatees is fieldwork? For our diorama (bottom) it was.

Canada lynx, on the other hand, are plentiful—in Canada and Alaska. In Colorado the animal is an endangered

A Colorado coyote family on a hot August afternoon

species. As of 1999, no confirmed lynx sightings had been made since 1973. To reestablish the lynx in its once native habitat, the Colorado Division of Wildlife began reintroducing them in 1999. Since then, more than seventy lynx have been transplanted from British Columbia, the Yukon Territory, and Alaska to Colorado's subalpine forests. Even if the controversial effort is successful, our diorama is still the closest look you'll ever get at this secretive feline.

Iñupiat children, Alaska, 1963

Over the years, Museum staff have had the opportunity to document cultures around the world while obtaining specimens for exhibits. On occasion these cultures were undergoing major change. While photographing and collecting animals for Bonfils Hall in 1963, one of our curators spent several days in the small Iñupiat village of Anaktuvuk, Alaska, north of the Arctic Circle. His visit occurred only three years after the natives began spending winters in the village, foregoing their nomadic existence so that their children could attend school. His photographs, now in our photo archives, preserve a small piece of their cultural history.

Each diorama depicts a particular place as it looked on a specific day. As fate would have it, the Sitka deer diorama shows Montague Island, Alaska, as it appeared in 1973—midway between two disasters. The painted background includes evidence of the 1964 Good Friday earthquake, which uplifted parts of the Alaskan coast thirty-five feet (11 m) and created tsunamis that leveled villages and forests. What is not shown is the disaster that

A native guide (left) displays the bull caribou collected in 1921 for our diorama (right).

befell this area a decade after the diorama's completion. In 1989, about seventy miles (113 km) off to the right, the tanker *Exxon Valdez* ran aground and dumped 11 million gallons of oil into Prince William Sound. Vagaries of wind and currents spared this coastline from the spill. The island across the way was not so fortunate. Our diorama preserves the once pristine appearance of this ecosystem.

The Things They'll Do . . .

Our exhibits staff have traditionally gone to great lengths to make our dioramas as realistic as possible. North American Wildlife includes several examples. A crew of six braved swarms of mosquitoes to collect 700 square feet (65 sq m) of Alaskan bog. They cut dense, soggy mats of moss into two-by-four-foot (0.6-by-1.2-m) strips (like sod), then bagged and shipped them via air freight to Denver. Back at the Museum the strips were fumigated, rehydrated to restore the moss's shape, dried, and then painted with twenty-three different shades to re-create the moss's original color. For other dioramas, staff made molds of a coyote den east

Tense standoff in the Far North: musk oxen and arctic wolves

Installing fake plants (inset); Museum party at the site depicted in the moose-caribou diorama, 1972

of Kiowa, Colorado, and rock formations and a ground squirrel burrow in Alaska's Tsusena Creek Valley to ensure their accurate appearance. They collected 1,700 square feet (158 sq m) of arctic tundra for the moose-caribou diorama. The background artist for the musk ox diorama even traveled to Ellesmere Island to view the light at midnight on the spring equinox (April 22), to capture the start of three months of continuous daylight. Such measures, though rarely obvious, help make it seem like pieces of the outdoors have been magically transported inside the building.

fun facts

- Our fifty-six-foot (17-m) fin whale skeleton graced California's famous Hotel del Coronado in the late 1800s before spending seventy-seven years at Colorado College in Colorado Springs. The college donated the whale to the DMNS in 1977.
- The moose-caribou diorama contains more than 1.3 million leaves.
- In 1921, a staff member ventured off alone across the vast Alaskan tundra to follow a caribou bull. He almost had to spend an October night in a newly acquired hide. The Moon finally appeared, allowing him to follow his tracks eight miles (13 km) back to his anxious guide.
- Exhibits staff made the trees in the Smoky Mountains diorama by covering tubes from rolls of carpet with bark and moss.

The moose half of our second largest diorama (inset); a young woman turns the tables on our photographer, 1921

Scenic Lounge

Take a break and enjoy the best view in Denver.

Overlooking City Park, the Denver skyline, and the majestic Rocky Mountains, our Scenic Lounge offers the best view in town. It's a great spot to sit and rest for a few minutes. Out the floor-to-ceiling windows you can see our prominent City Park

The view from the Museum

Both people and Canada geese visit City Park, the Museum's home since 1901.

neighbors: Ferril Lake, the red-roofed City Park Pavilion (built in 1896) on the opposite side of the lake, and off to the right, the Denver Zoo. On warm summer days, you can watch kids frolicking in the City Park Interactive Water Feature. Built in 1999, its 64 jets shoot water up into the air from a granite plaza, creating shimmering waves, curtains, and geysers, which come splashing down on the youngsters running across it.

North American Indian Cultures

Mary W. A. and Francis V. Crane American Indian Hall

Visit the homes of North America's Indians to discover the variety of ways in which they live.

North American Indian Cultures shows how each group of Native Americans has historically dealt with the same challenge—thriving in a particular environment. For hundreds of years, Native Americans have lived in places as diverse as frigid arctic coastlines, sizzling southwestern deserts, and shady eastern woodlands. As you wander through Crane Hall, you can see how they gathered, cultivated, and hunted food and built shelters, using the resources provided by their environment. You can actually "visit" their varied homes: an Eskimo snowhouse, a Northwest Coast clan house, a Navajo hogan, a Hopi stone-and-adobe house, a Cheyenne tipi, and a Miccosukee camp.

Displayed in these re-creations and nearby are the objects of their everyday and ceremonial lives—clothing, tools, storage containers, saddles, boats, jewelry, cradles, toys. Exquisite beadwork or quillwork, distinctive designs, and fine craftsmanship make many of them beautiful as well as functional. American Indians made these objects from a wide variety of plant, animal, and mineral materials. Years later (in most instances), these objects show us how these diverse people lived. Some tribes hunted big game; others survived on small game and the edible plants they gathered; still others settled in villages and farmed clearings in forests.

Crane Hall boasts the only two life-size dioramas in the Museum featuring human beings and cultural materials. In one, a young visitor arrives at a Cheyenne encampment in the 1860s. The scene occurs just twenty miles (32 km) east of the Museum, along Coal Creek, on a site where real artifacts were discovered. In the other diorama,

Cheyenne ceramic plate

Local Cheyenne Indians, such as the girl at left, served as models for our Cheyenne diorama.

a Miccosukee father returns home after poling his dugout canoe miles to the general store for a few staples. The scene takes place in Florida's Everglades, some forty miles (64 km) west of Miami, about 1950. Members of the Cheyenne and Miccosukee tribes served as models for the mannequins and assisted in the dioramas' creation. In fact, an advisory group of Native Americans helped Museum staff develop all of Crane Hall's exhibits. The group reviewed labels and objects to ensure that their people's histories are correctly interpreted.

Although much of the exhibition focuses on the past, woven throughout are ways in which modern Native Americans are keeping their cultures strong. Contemporary native-made objects, photographs, and videos demonstrate that many American Indians continue to observe their peoples' traditions. Various tribes are also helping the Museum comply with the Native American Graves Protection and Repatriation Act of 1990. As tribes identify objects they consider sacred

Northwest Coast totem poles

or patrimonial (belonging to the whole tribe), the objects are removed from display and may eventually be returned to the tribes. The dialogue involved renews the relationship between the Museum and native peoples, with both sides sharing a common goal of preserving American Indian cultures.

Navajo ceramic jar

Two Cranes to Build One Hall

North American Indian Cultures owes its existence largely to Mary and Francis Crane. From 1951 to 1968, the Cranes collected some 14,000 Native American and Mesoamerican artifacts, purchased from other collectors, reservation artists and trading posts, dealers, and galleries. They displayed their treasures in their Southeast Museum of the North American Indian in Marathon, Florida, a hundred miles (160 km) south of Miami. When the Cranes decided to find a new home for their collection in 1968, they chose Denver.

Thanks to the Cranes' donation, the DMNS went overnight from having a minuscule collection of North American ethnographic materials to owning the largest such collection between Chicago and Los Angeles. Museum staff traveled to Florida to help fill four moving vans with boxed and crated objects. The Cranes' valuable collection of Precolumbian gold traveled separately under high security. The gold was carefully packed into two beat-up suitcases, tied up with rope, and loaded into a station wagon for the drive back to Denver. Whenever the three couriers stopped to eat, they drew straws to see who would stay in the car with the gold.

Crane Hall opened in phases from 1974 through 1978. Since then, staff have added new interpretive panels to certain sections and rotated objects on and off display to ensure their long-term preservation. Like the cultures it depicts, Crane Hall constantly evolves while remaining true to its heritage.

Hopi kachina doll

Sioux beaded horse hood

fun facts

- The miniature diorama of a Northwest Coast potlatch celebration depicts one of the hall's benefactors, Mary Crane, dressed as an 1890s missionary. She's the one with white hair.
- Two of the four totem poles at the hall's entrance were displayed outside the Museum from 1923 to 1968.
- A Navajo medicine man performed a Blessing Way Ceremony for the hogan before its debut in 1989.
- The local Cheyenne woman who served as the model for the seated grandmother in the diorama made the clothes that her figure wears.

Australia and South Pacific Islands

Journey to lands down under to see unique wildlife and contrasting landscapes.

Australia broke apart from the rest of the world's landmasses 130 to 65 million years ago, and it's quite evident that evolution took a different path there, thanks to the geographic isolation. Australia now boasts animals found nowhere else in the world: koalas, emus, red kangaroos, cassowaries, duck-billed platypuses, kookaburras, Lumholtz's tree kangaroos, lyrebirds. You can see all of them in this hall, along with dramatic evidence of Australia's varied landscapes. Within this continent the size of the continental United States lie eucalyptus forests, home of tree ferns and towering mountain ashes; a huge central desert; and lush rainforests with vine-covered trees. The five dioramas will give you a real appreciation for the diversity of life and landforms in the land down under.

Painting a background, ca. 1962

The other half of the hall highlights two Pacific Ocean islands. Two dioramas depict scenes on Campbell Island, located in the subantarctic some 400 miles (640 km) south of New Zealand. One diorama *(above)* features the wildlife that frequent the island's beaches—giant elephant seals, smaller fur seals, and three species of penguins, the island's chief bird inhabitants. The other takes you to the island's heights, the nesting site of the royal albatross. These large birds land on Campbell Island once every two years to mate and raise their young.

The third diorama depicts Laysan Island, a tiny sanctuary in the Hawaiian archipelago for thousands of seabirds. The diorama includes nineteen bird species that make use of Laysan's limited space. Just over a century ago, five bird species lived only on this island. Then a well-intentioned individual introduced rabbits—future food for shipwrecked sailors. The rabbits multiplied and denuded the island of vegetation, wiping out one of the rare birds, the flightless Laysan rail. In 1912, former director Alfred M. Bailey joined a U.S. Biological Survey effort to destroy the rabbits. He was able to collect a couple of Laysan rails. This diorama represents one of the few places you can still see this now extinct species.

Expeditions to the Other Side of the World

Director Bailey often said that fieldwork was the "lifeblood" of a natural history museum. That was certainly true for this hall. It took five expeditions over ten years to collect the materials for these eight dioramas.

The Australian dioramas resulted from cooperative efforts among the DMNS; the National Museum of Victoria in Melbourne, Australia; and the Australian government. Our first two-man expedition in 1949 teamed up with a dozen staff members from the National Museum. For four months they collected zoological specimens across Australia. Two of our staff returned in 1952 to gather botanical materials for the foregrounds. Additional trips in 1954 and 1958 provided photographic studies to aid in the completion of the dioramas—America's first large displays of Australian habitats—which were dedicated in 1959.

Because of its remote location, the fieldwork for the Campbell Island dioramas had to be completed in one trip. In early 1958, the Museum's five-man party sailed from New Zealand aboard a U.S. Navy destroyer escort ship, the only transportation available. Their supplies—food, lumber, salt, and plaster—had

Sketching an albatross, 1958 (right), for our diorama

been delivered in advance by the ship that resupplied the island's weather station once a year. At the time, ten meteorologists were the sole human inhabitants. For six cold, wet weeks, our field crew and three Kiwi colleagues studied some of the island's thousands of wild inhabitants. The party photographed the flora and fauna; collected birds, mammals, plant life, and rocks; and sketched the wildlife and scenery. When the Navy ship returned to pick them up, they worried that the longest part of the 9,000-mile (14,500-km) journey to Denver would be the mile between the dock and the ship in an open boat—with six weeks' worth of precious specimens aboard. Fortunately, calm weather prevailed, and both the field party and the specimens made it safely back to the Museum.

The Australian desert diorama (above); an Aboriginal hunting party, 1949 (left); director Bailey with a joey, 1949 (right)

The fruits of their fieldwork were unveiled to the public in 1966.

Today Campbell Island has been left to the animals. The weather station was automated in 1995, so now the only humans there are visitors—tourists from cruise ships and researchers. The New Zealand government limits access to the island, one of the country's national nature reserves, and carefully monitors human impacts, seeking to preserve Campbell Island's unique plant life and abundance and diversity of seabirds.

Australia's famous koalas

fun facts

- The Museum had a permit to collect one male elephant seal on Campbell Island, so in the diorama only one bull is a taxidermy mount. The other is a fiberglass model.
- The Aborigines painted into the background of the Australian desert diorama were the first humans to appear in a Museum background.
- In the Campbell Island dioramas, the background paintings extend onto the floor—one of the artist's innovations.

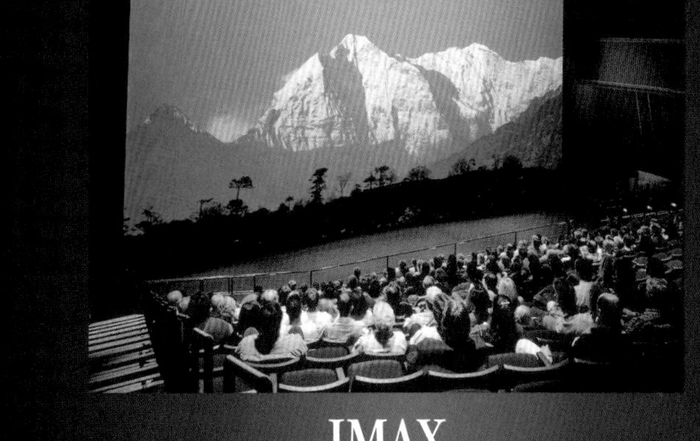

IMAX

Lawrence C. Phipps IMAX Theater

Experience the world's biggest movie adventures!

If only every movie theater could be like this one. The four-and-a-half-story tall screen literally fills your eye to the max. The film that's projected *(right)* is four times the size of standard movie film *(lower right)*, making for incredibly sharp pictures. Fifty-eight speakers surround you with digital sound, and there's not a bad seat in the house.

The films in our 440-seat IMAX theater transport you to spectacular sites and exciting adventures the world over. Consider the five most popular films to have graced our screen: *Everest, The Living Sea, The Dream Is Alive* (filmed aboard the space shuttle), *Antarctica,* and *Ring of Fire* (all about volcanoes).

The film for a typical movie sits on a four-foot-wide (1.2-m) horizontal platter and weighs about 250 pounds

Phipps Auditorium, 1940, the beginning of its years as a multipurpose theater

As a member of the Museum Film Network, the DMNS helped fund the climbing expedition that filmed the hit movie Everest.

(113 kg). Nearly two-and-a-half miles (4 km) of film feed through the 1,100-pound (500-kg) projector in forty-five minutes. You can see this all for yourself. Just peek through the projection booth window at the very back of the theater as you leave.

From 1940 to 1982, this space had a glorious run as Phipps Auditorium. Millions of people filled its 950 seats for programs sponsored by the Museum and other organizations: travel films, lectures, Saturday morning nature films and cartoons for kids, concerts, church group meetings, national conventions, and even accordion recitals. Phipps Auditorium was transformed into the world's twelfth IMAX theater in 1983.

Even elephants appear larger than life on our huge screen.

Exhibits

Floor 3

Clockwise from top: Stegosaurus *and* Allosaurus; *ancient Egyptian coffin; small moth on wild rose next to Colorado columbine*

Egyptian Mummies

Helen K. and Arthur E. Johnson Foundation Exhibit Gallery

Unravel the secrets buried with our mummies.

Egyptian Mummies reveals how and why the ancient Egyptians mummified their dead. At the center of the exhibition are the mummies of two Egyptian women, both of whom died about 3,000 years ago. One was apparently a moderately wealthy woman, for she was properly mummified and wrapped with lots of good quality linen. Several amulets lie inside her wrappings, which are covered with a layer of resin. The other woman was considerably less affluent. She was poorly mummified and carelessly wrapped in a few sheets of linen. You can even see her face because the wrappings around her head have been removed, probably within the last hundred years.

For more than three millennia, ancient Egyptians believed that a person who died could go on to a second, eternal life in a place much like Egypt—only better. There the deceased would join Osiris, the god of the afterlife. The person needed, however, to use his or her original body in the afterlife. To preserve the body for eternity, priests removed the internal organs, dried the body, then wrapped it and placed it in a coffin. You can see the process illustrated alongside an embalmer's tools. The gallery also includes artifacts from tombs, animal mummies, and a large scale model of an Egyptian temple.

Both mummies are displayed with painted, wooden coffins. Somehow the "rich woman's mummy" wound up in a common man's coffin.

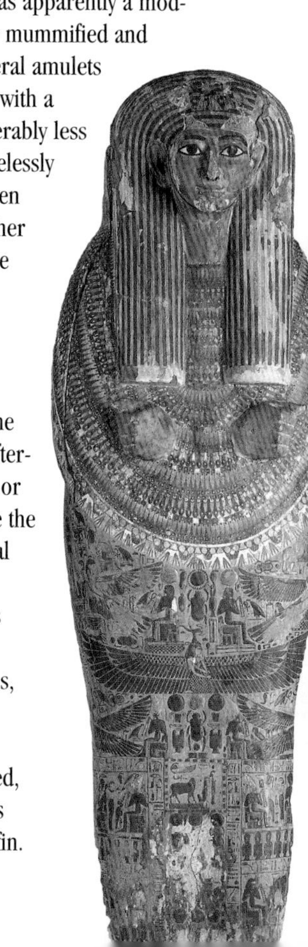

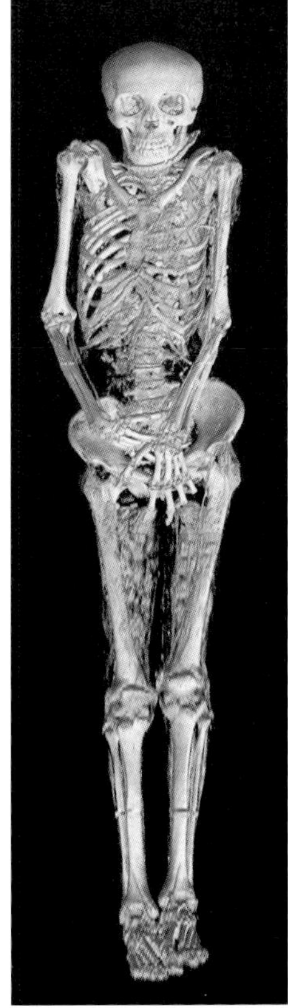

Three views of the "poor woman's mummy" (from left): coffin lid; outer wrappings and exposed head; rendering of her skeleton based on data from CT scans. Hieroglyphs on one coffin lid (opposite; details below) indicate it belonged to a priest.

We don't know how. The two were purchased together a century ago, so perhaps a switch occurred then. It's also possible that the woman was moved out of her own coffin in ancient times. The coffin with the "poor woman's mummy" is covered with a layer of bitumen, a natural asphalt, that obscures the pictures and hieroglyphs on it. A nearby reproduction, built in 1994 by our Egyptian Study Society, shows what it probably looked like when it was new.

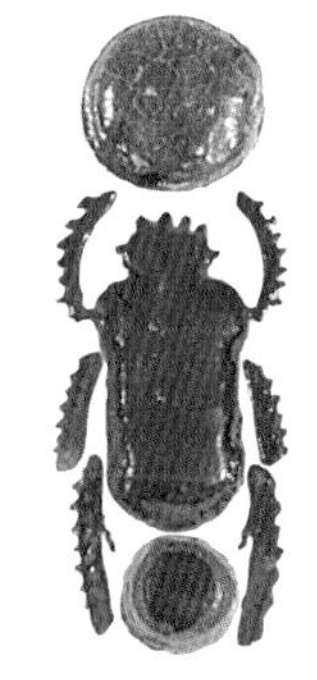

Our two mummies left Egypt the same way many others did: They were sold as souvenirs to a tourist, a practice allowed by the Egyptian government until 1946. A wealthy businessman from Pueblo, Colorado, purchased these mummies in 1904 while touring the world. He shipped them back to his hometown, where they were displayed for a number of years. Now owned by the City of Pueblo, the mummies were loaned to the DMNS by their caretakers, Pueblo's Rosemount Museum, so that more people could see and learn from them.

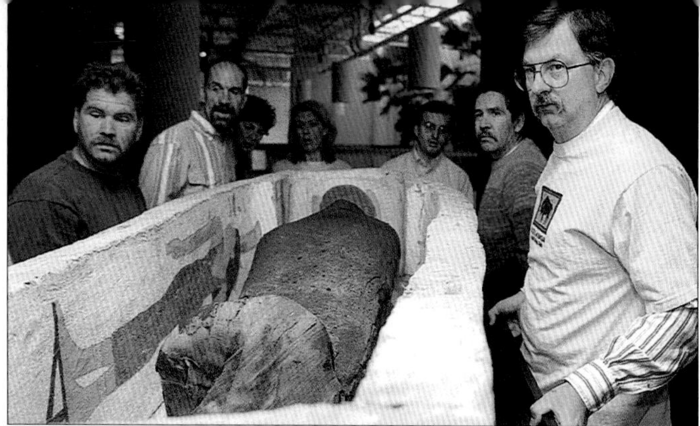

How many Museum staff does it take to move a mummy? About a dozen.

Looking Inside the Mummies

The "Look Inside the Mummies" section of the exhibition shows you science in progress—research done by Museum staff with the help of local institutions. In 1991, a Museum anthropologist teamed up with medical doctors and scientists from the University of Colorado Health Sciences Center (UCHSC) and University Hospital to study the two human mummies. After transporting each "patient" to the hospital by ambulance, the researchers used X rays and Computed Tomography, commonly known as CT or a CAT scan, to look inside the mummies. The tests produced detailed insights into how these women were mummified. You can see the test results for yourself on the giant hospital clipboards, or you can look over the scientists' shoulders as they decipher the CT scans in the exhibit video.

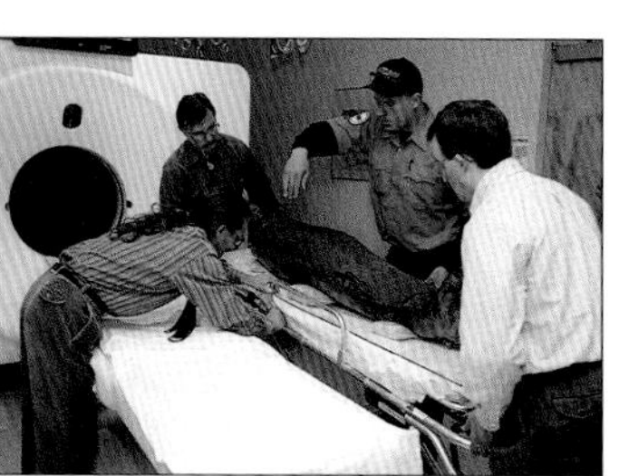

CAT-scanning a mummy, 1998

Scanning the mummies was just a first step. Staff at the Center for Human Simulation at UCHSC then transformed the CT data into incredible images of the mummies' skeletons. To do so, they used technology from Pixar, the same company that produces Disney's computer-animated films. For the rich woman's mummy, the resulting images showed not just her skeleton but also the funerary objects—a scarab, gold foil covering the embalmer's incision, and a metal object—hidden beneath her wrappings. The identity and significance of the metal object remain a mystery.

Thanks to modern medical technology, we have been able to learn a great deal about these mummies, all without removing a single wrapping. Such noninvasive techniques help us ensure that the mummies will be around for future generations of scientists and Museum visitors.

Looks like new because it is! Reproduction coffin built by our Egyptian Study Society; poor woman's mummy (inset)

fun facts

- Advances in technology: When the rich woman's mummy was CAT-scanned in 1998, it took four hours to scan her every one millimeter (about 1/32 of an inch) from head to toe. A less detailed scan in 1991 took ten hours to complete.
- This exhibition opened on the first floor in 1998. It moved to its current location in 2000 to make room for the space science exhibition.
- *Egyptian Mummies* won a first-place award in the 1999 American Association of Museums Exhibition Competition.

Prehistoric Journey

Travel 3.5 billion years through the history of life on Earth—from the beginning of life through the time of the dinosaurs to the modern world.

Prehistoric Journey transports you back in time to view the incredible story of life on Earth. You begin your journey in the Time-Travel Theater, which recounts the 3 billion years that the first life-forms (single-celled bacteria) had the planet to themselves. From there you follow a trail through time that features seven stunning reconstructions of prehistoric habitats. Each one depicts a critical turning point in the history of life. Off the beaten path are "evidence areas," where more than 530 spectacular fossils show how paleontologists know what Earth, its animals, and plants looked like millions of years ago. At three points along the main trail, time stations set the stage for the next chunk of Earth's history and illustrate the immensity of geologic time.

The habitat reconstructions exemplify the Museum's tradition of creating meticulously detailed dioramas. Museum staff selected seven sites, mostly in North America, with unusually high abundances of various fossils. Crews then excavated both plant and animal fossils and carefully studied the geology at each site. This fieldwork enabled our scientists and exhibits staff to reconstruct the plants, animals, and the actual topography of the site. Thus, each diorama depicts a specific fossil place at a certain point in Earth's history—not a compilation of fossils from many sites and times.

Touching up a pelycosaur

Starting down the trail through time, you come to the "Early Life" section of the exhibition. The first diorama, the Ancient Sea Floor, features the first multicellular life, which evolved about 600 million years ago. These life-forms may have been large compared to bacteria, but they were still quite simple compared to modern life-forms. Fossil evidence of these creatures, which you can examine in the evidence area, came from the Ediacara Hills in the desert of South Australia. You can also see the actual apparatus that Stanley Miller and Harold Urey used in 1953 to create the building blocks of life in the laboratory.

Life Diversifies, Conquers Land, and Takes to the Air

By 425 million years ago, life in the sea had become much more varied and complex, as shown in "Diversity in the Sea," *Prehistoric Journey*'s next section. The colorful Sea Lily Reef diorama depicts an early coral reef teeming with life. The reef animals depended on each other for shelter and food. In the evidence area, you can see the limestone quarry in Racine, Wisconsin, that preserved these creatures for millions of years, as well as exquisite fossils of sea lilies, trilobites, sea scorpions, and cephalopods (squid relatives).

Cone-shaped cephalopods (left) cruise over the Sea Lily Reef in search of prey.

As you climb the stairs (or ride the elevator), you are metaphorically "Leaving the Water" and now find yourself at Between Two Worlds. In this diorama, primitive plants and arthropods, such as scorpions, move onto land 395 million years ago, colonizing a shore that became Wyoming's Beartooth and Bighorn Mountains. The nearby cases illustrate how organisms evolved ways to survive in this new environment, and they explain how evolution works. Playing the Natural Selection Computer Game is a great way to see evolution "in action."

"Forests and Flight" highlights the first forests of early conifers, seed ferns, and telephone pole–like lycopod trees, and the early land animals that inhabited them. Its centerpiece is the Kansas Coastline diorama. The dramatic, two-story re-creation of a 295-million-year-old coastal stream features amphibians, finbacked protomammals, and gigantic insects, among them dragonflies with two-foot (0.6-m) wingspans. Dragonflies and other insects were the first animals to fly. In the evidence area, you can learn more about the Hamilton, Kansas, cow pasture where fossil evidence for the scene was found and find out about the greatest mass extinction of all time, when 96 percent of Earth's species vanished.

"Time of the Dinosaurs"

Descending the stairs, you step into a scene from 66 million years ago: the Cretaceous Creekbed, one of the Museum's first "enviroramas"—dioramas you can walk through, complete with sound and light effects. Two male bony-headed dinosaurs battle for the attention of a nearby female. A *Triceratops* skull rots in a flowing stream, while small mammals scurry through the forest underbrush. Listen carefully and you'll hear snapping tree branches that signal the approach of a *Tyrannosaurus rex.* During the time

Dimetrodon, *a finbacked protomammal, attacks a large amphibian; fossil fern (above).*

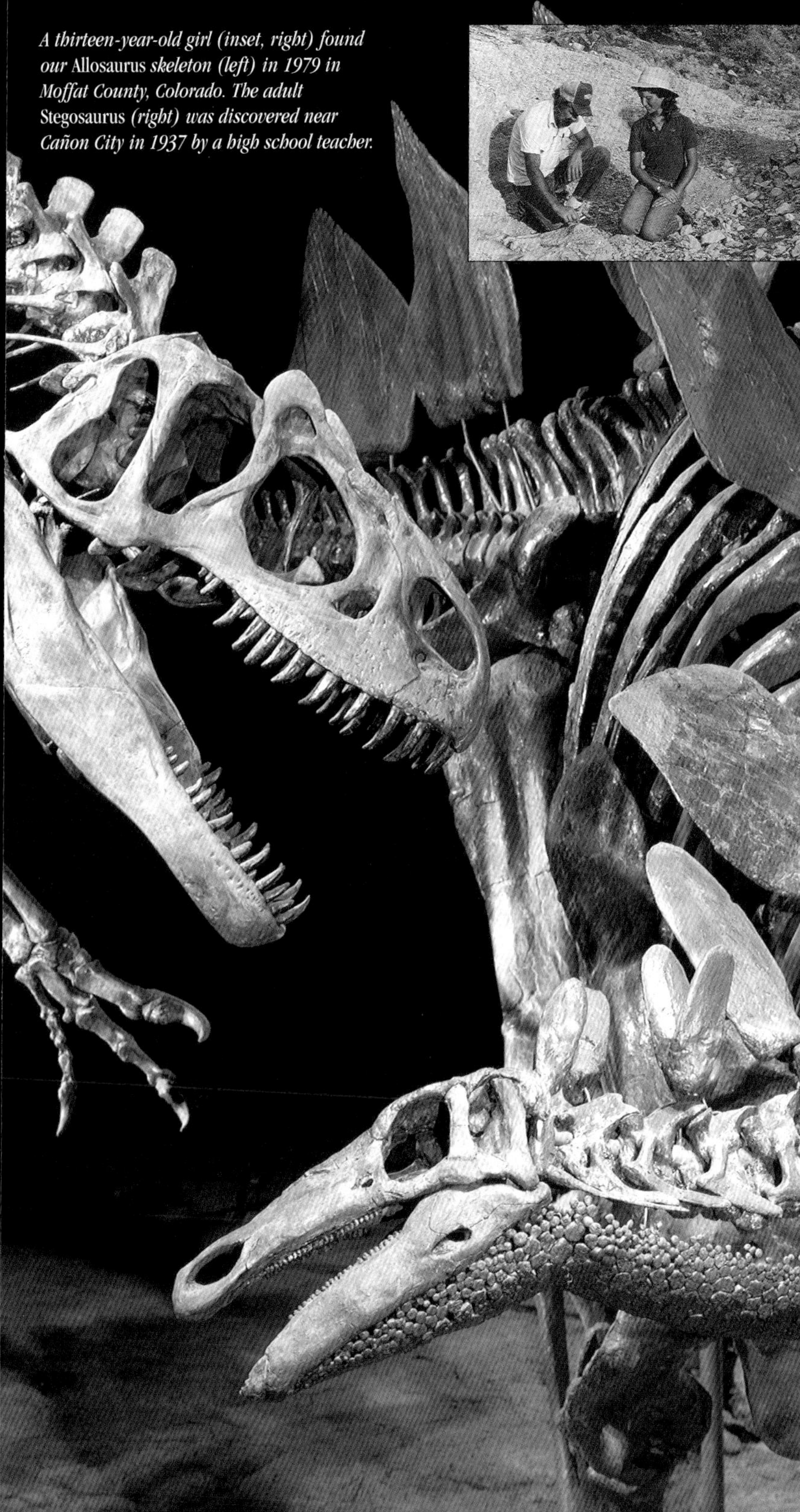

A thirteen-year-old girl (inset, right) found our Allosaurus *skeleton (left) in 1979 in Moffat County, Colorado. The adult* Stegosaurus *(right) was discovered near Cañon City in 1937 by a high school teacher.*

Insets: Featured fossils include rare baby stegosaurs (left) and skulls of T. rex *and other dinosaurs (right). Above, several* Coelophysis *flee from a crocodile-like phytosaur.*

of the last dinosaurs, the badlands near Marmarth, North Dakota, certainly looked a lot different.

The spacious evidence area features skeletons of fifteen dinosaurs. Among them are the first articulated *Coelophysis* skeletons in the world; an eighty-foot-long (24-m) *Diplodocus;* a fierce *Allosaurus* attacking a mother *Stegosaurus* and her young; and a duck-billed *Edmontosaurus* with a *T. rex* bite out of its tail. Unlike the *Diplodocus*'s first-floor home, where the Museum's dinosaurs lived from the 1930s until 1994, here there's enough room for its entire fifty-foot (15-m) tail. In the shadow of these impressive creatures, you can investigate whether dinosaurs were warm- or cold-blooded, touch real dinosaur bones, and learn about some dinosaurs' parenting skills.

Dinosaurs shared their world with the first mammals, birds, and flowers, as well as other reptiles. The last section of the evidence area includes fabulous fossils of flying reptiles; marine reptiles, such as mosasaurs, ichthyosaurs, and turtles; fish; and other marine creatures, including stunning iridescent ammonites. A re-creation of the Cretaceous-Tertiary (K-T) boundary—the geologic marker of the extinction of the dinosaurs—and a video about that catastrophic event finish off the "Time of the Dinosaurs."

The Rise of Mammals and the Modern World

With dinosaurs out of the way, many new kinds of mammals evolved, taking advantage of newly available habitats and food sources. Among them were early lemurlike primates, such as those in the Rainforest Treetop diorama in "Tropical Rockies." These animals lived 50 million years ago, at a time when Lost Cabin, Wyoming, was a tropical rainforest. Showcased near the diorama are dozens of fossils from this time period: fossil palm leaves uncovered during the construction of Denver International Airport; intricate fossils of fish and leaves; and complete skeletons of rhinoceroses and rhinolike titanotheres. You can see for yourself that mammals were getting bigger. They were also getting faster (thanks to the evolution of hooves) and becoming more social, living in herds for the first time.

As you enter the Nebraska Woodland envirorama, you come between a 20-million-year-old predator and its prey. A large *Dinohyus* (nicknamed the Terminator Pig by staff) has caught sight of three small gazelle camels. Fossil evidence for this scene from Agate Springs, Nebraska, indicates that, by this time, the climate had cooled, and the dense rainforests had given way to a more open landscape. The evidence area shows how mammals

If Dinohyus *were alive, you'd be close enough to smell its breath.*

A reconstruction of human ancestor Lucy steps down from the trees both literally and figuratively. It took the artist who created her fifteen months to reconstruct her skeleton, muscles, and features, and attach almost a million hairs onto her body.

adapted to the new grasslands. You can trace the evolution of horses and marvel at the long-jawed elephant, giant bison, and mammoth that used to call North America home. A final alcove documents the relatively recent evolution of our species. The exhibit features an incredibly lifelike re-creation of Lucy, the 3.2-million-year-old *Australopithecus afarensis*, perhaps the most famous of all human ancestors. A nearby case holds an artifact ranked as one of the twentieth century's ten most significant archaeological discoveries: the Folsom point. Museum staff found it near Folsom, New Mexico, in 1926. Its existence proved that humans came to North America thousands of years earlier than previously believed.

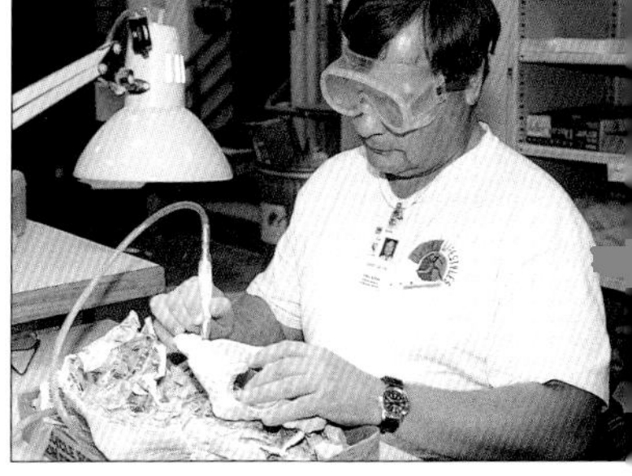

Volunteer fossil preparator at work

Your prehistoric journey ends at the Schlessman Family Foundation Earth Sciences Laboratory. Here, Museum staff and volunteers use tools such as dental picks, air scribes, and paintbrushes to free fossils from their plaster-and-rock casings. Our preparators' efforts produced many of the magnificent fossil specimens in *Prehistoric Journey*. You can watch and even discuss their work with them, as they continually seek to decipher the mysteries of past life on Earth.

Edmontosaurus *in the old dinosaur hall, 1936*

- In 1936, *Edmontosaurus* became the Museum's first dinosaur on display. It remains one of the best of its kind ever discovered.
- *Prehistoric Journey* took six years and $7.7 million to create. It opened in 1995 and received the American Association of Museums 1996 award for best exhibition.
- At a 1995 symposium, renowned author Dr. Stephen Jay Gould pronounced *Prehistoric Journey* "the best prehistoric life exhibit in the world."
- If Earth's history were condensed into one day, and Earth formed at 12:01 A.M., humans wouldn't appear until less than a minute before midnight.

Rare Birds

Ellen M. Standley Hall

Get a good close look at birds you probably wouldn't—or can't—see in the wild.

Rare Birds highlights species that few people get to see—either because of where the birds live or how few of them are left. Along the hall's north wall are the birds of the Far North. Twenty-eight different species in four dioramas illustrate the avian diversity that exists during this region's brief summer nesting season. The center two dioramas depict eider ducks in the Bering Strait and geese, swans, cranes, and songbirds on the Alaskan tundra. The outer two show seabirds—puffins, gannets, auks, and murres—nesting on the crowded, steep cliffs of Fairway Rock, Alaska *(above),* and Bonaventure Island, Quebec. Most of

This 1946 photograph (left) shows how accurately our diorama depicts Bonaventure Island.

Now appearing only in museums: The last passenger pigeon died in 1914.

these specimens (the Bering Strait group excepted) were collected on Museum expeditions between 1921 and 1924. The dioramas debuted to the public in 1940.

The four dioramas along the south wall feature five species that are either extremely rare or extinct. Museum staff installed the dioramas from 1945 to 1948 using specimens that other individuals collected decades earlier, when the birds were more plentiful. In fact, the passenger pigeons and whooping cranes date back to the 1880s and 1890s. Of the five species featured, two—the Carolina parakeet and the passenger pigeon—have vanished forever. The ivory-billed woodpecker teeters at the brink of extinction, with only a few possibly surviving in Cuba. Thanks to intensive recovery efforts, however, the California condor and the whooping crane are slowly making a comeback. With the continued success of captive breeding and reintroduction programs, perhaps someday these two species will no longer be considered rare.

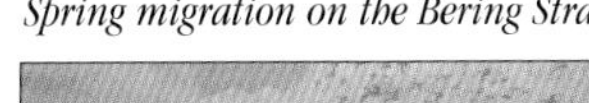

Spring migration on the Bering Strait

- One of the six Carolina parakeets is a wooden, painted sculpture.
- The California condor diorama is the only one in the Museum with a hole cut in the floor so that the background painting can extend lower.

Explore Colorado: From Plains to Peaks

Walter C. Mead Ecological Hall

Discover the diversity of Colorado's ecosystems and the wildlife that inhabits them.

Explore Colorado: From Plains to Peaks takes you on a tour of the state's ecosystems, featured in eleven beautiful dioramas. Driving from the grassland prairies through shrublands and forests to the high alpine tundra would take hours. Here you can see them all in minutes, along with some of the state's most interesting birds and small mammals.

Your tour guide is a talented naturalist named C. Moore. The central kiosk introduces you to C. Moore, Colorado's topography and ecosystems, and some basic principles of ecology. Interpretive panels at each diorama include identifications of the plants and animals, information about the ecosystem—its characteristic vegetation and climate and where to find it in Colorado—and a page from C. Moore's field notebook. C. Moore's sketches, photographs, and easy-to-read observations convey the naturalist's excitement and concerns about the species and scenes depicted.

Starting with a scene of the Arizona desert in rare but spectacular full bloom (the only non-Colorado diorama in the hall), you circle to the left, exploring seven of Colorado's eight ecosystems. An ecosystem is a recognizable landscape of plants, animals, and environmental conditions, and the interactions between them. Your stops include a warm, dry piñon-juniper woodland, home of piñon pines and gnarled junipers, and the cliffside nest of golden eagles. The plains grassland diorama, *Explore Colorado*'s largest, features the teeming bird life of Pawnee National Grassland, where the native grasses that once covered eastern Colorado still grow wild.

Yellow-rumped warbler

A characteristic swath of alpine tundra near Long's Peak

Phoebus parnassian butterfly

From here, you ascend to higher elevations. You see great blue herons nesting along the South Platte River in a riparian land ecosystem and male sage grouse strutting their stuff in a semidesert shrubland. Two dioramas depict Colorado's montane shrublands, with Gambel oaks ablaze in autumn red and wild turkeys foraging for food. In the cool, wet subalpine forest, you find summer wildflowers among the spruce, fir, and aspen trees, and at the highest edge of the subalpine forest you come to treeline, the point above which no trees can grow. Finally you reach the cold, harsh world of the alpine tundra, where marmots and pikas scurry about on the brief summer carpet of wildflowers.

The subalpine forest diorama features Colorado's famous aspen trees.

You'll find piñon-juniper woodlands like this one in western Colorado.

Other exhibit highlights include historical photographs of the hall, discovery boxes that light up beneath each diorama, and an interactive video that lets you build an ecosystem or experience the sights and sounds of nature. To complete your tour of Colorado ecosystems, check out the mule deer dioramas in *Edge of the Wild* on the second floor. Mule deer live among the evergreens and aspens of Colorado's montane forests. With this extra stop you will have fully explored Colorado's ecosystems—all without leaving the building.

New Life for an Old Hall

Mead Hall has been an exhibit gallery since the Museum opened to the public in 1908. For its first twenty-eight years, light from windows illuminated the hall's cases of birds and bird eggs, and an open well in the middle of this hall allowed natural light to reach the second floor. Then in 1936, the Museum began to modernize its exhibits. With the windows and well covered, Mead Hall became the Museum's first exhibit hall to have modern dioramas installed—with curved backgrounds, domed ceilings, tilted glass windows, and fluorescent lights. Workers from the Works Progress Administration created the thousands of accessories (fake plants) needed to fill the eleven dioramas. The hall was finished in 1944.

Extensive renovations transformed Mead Hall into *Explore Colorado* in 1991. The two-year, $850,000 project, funded by the Scientific and Cultural Facilities District, improved the hall's appearance and restored the original molded plaster ceiling. More important, staff and volunteers cleaned and refurbished the dioramas and added new interpretive panels.

Discovery boxes below each diorama are a big hit with kids of all ages.

As part of the interpretation process, local scientists, led by a Museum zoologist, reassessed how we think about Colorado. After collecting data and observing changes in vegetation all over the state, they developed a simple yet accurate approach to classifying Colorado's ecosystems. Defined largely by dominant plants, the eight ecosystems reflect the realities of nature and of Colorado's varied topography. Although originally developed for this exhibition, the classifications have since been adopted by organizations and government agencies statewide. *Explore Colorado* provides a great example of how Museum research can benefit not only visitors but also the local and scientific communities.

Cases of birds line the hall in 1909.

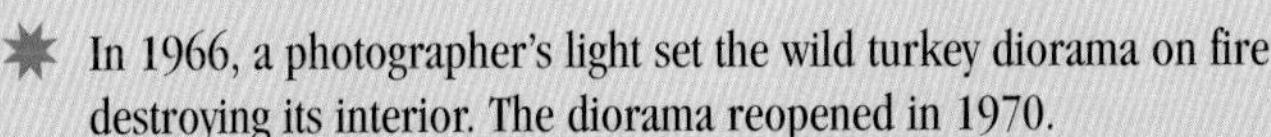

- In 1966, a photographer's light set the wild turkey diorama on fire, destroying its interior. The diorama reopened in 1970.

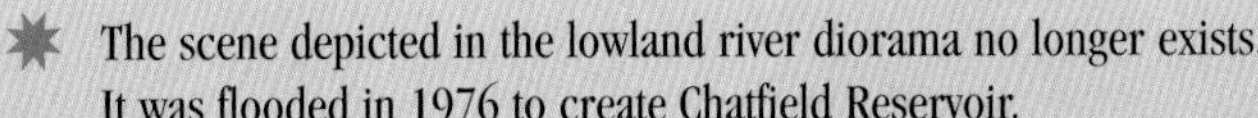

- The scene depicted in the lowland river diorama no longer exists. It was flooded in 1976 to create Chatfield Reservoir.

- The photograph of C. Moore's desk shows field notebooks from the 1930s and pictures of the 1990–1991 renovation team, the exhibition's curator in the field, and the exhibit designer's dog.

- *Explore Colorado* won the 1992 American Association of Museums Curators' Committee Exhibition Competition.

Birds

William H. James Memorial Hall

Go bird-watching indoors.

Ringing James Hall are nine dioramas showing birds from Colorado, elsewhere in North America, and South America in their natural habitats. Four depict scenes in the Centennial State. Majestic bald eagles fish along the Platte River. Sandhill cranes stop near Alamosa to rest and find a mate, just as thousands of the birds do each spring. Also featured are flocks of mallard and pintail ducks in Weld County and prairie chickens on their "booming" (mating) grounds near Wray.

Three dioramas portray scenes in the southern United States and in Mexico. Blue and snow geese come in for a landing in a Missouri wildlife refuge. In Florida, a great white heron takes off past a crocodile and a diamond-back rattlesnake locked in mortal combat. Boobies and other seabirds present a more peaceful scene as they crowd onto their nesting sites on Isabela Island, off the west coast of Mexico.

Look out below! Blue and snow geese

The last two dioramas resulted from the Museum's second expedition to South America and its first to Central America. Director Jesse Figgins and another staff member secured the hoatzins and scarlet ibises for one diorama in Guyana (which was then British Guiana) in 1928. A two-man expedition traveled to Guatemala in late 1935, where they collected numerous plant and bird species

Looking pretty good for their age, these scarlet ibis specimens are more than seventy years old.

for the lush, tropical cloud forest diorama. (The cloud forest gets its name from being at an elevation of 10,000 feet [3,048 m].) Among the colorful avian inhabitants of this diorama are long-tailed quetzals *(opposite, top)*, the national bird of Guatemala.

- Our Central American expedition sailed from New Orleans in 1935 aboard a "United Fruit Liner."
- Alfred M. Bailey's account of the collecting expedition to Isabela Island, Mexico, appeared in the September 1941 issue of *National Geographic*.

Botswana: Safari to Wild Africa

Helen K. and Arthur E. Johnson Botswana Africa Hall

Take an imaginary safari to one of Africa's last wildlife refuges.

B*otswana: Safari to Wild Africa* transports you to one of the few places you can still see immense concentrations of wildlife. Located in southern Africa, Botswana claims habitats ranging from desert to savanna to woodlands to swamp. Large numbers of animals inhabit them all, but especially those that provide precious water. Five of the hall's eight dioramas depict sites in the northern third of Botswana, where the Linyanti-Chobe and Okavango Rivers flow year-round.

The Okavango River pours its contents into the huge Okavango Delta in northwestern Botswana. This permanently flooded land is home to a variety of wildlife, as shown in three dioramas. In one, two sitatungas follow a hippo path toward the river's edge. Sitatungas wouldn't normally get this close to a Nile crocodile, but the pairing mirrors the predator-prey relationship frozen in time across the way, where a cheetah chases bounding impalas across the savanna at the southern end of the delta *(above)*. The third Okavango scene depicts two red lechwe sparring over prime

Gathering at the ol' watering hole: Savuti Crossroads diorama

Lions laze around after a big meal.

waterside territory as a waterbuck passes by on its way to drink. The interpretive panels beneath each diorama identify the bird and plant life. Look for yellow dots on the maps to see the exact location of each scene.

Botswana's Chobe National Park provides settings for two dioramas. In one, a pride of lions rests in the shade after satiating themselves at a kill. Stretched across the hall's back wall is the Savuti Crossroads diorama. At ninety-two feet (28 m) wide and thirty-five feet (11 m) deep, it ranks as the Museum's largest diorama. The expansive scene illustrates the array of animals that gathers at a small water hole during the dry season—warthogs, sable antelope, Plains zebras, steenboks, red-billed francolins, Chacma baboons, greater kudus, a rufus-crowned roller, elephants, wildebeests, and ostriches.

Three dioramas portray the land that covers two-thirds of Botswana—the Kalahari Desert. Gemsboks, springboks, and red hartebeests have adapted to this "land of great thirst," as illustrated in the large habitat diorama. Two smaller dioramas and a separate case portray the nocturnal animals of the Kalahari. In these dimly lit scenes, a leopard hauls its prey (a duiker) up into a tree, and three unusual-looking mammals (an aardwolf, aardvark, and Cape pangolin) search for a midnight snack of termites.

Other cases in the hall provide an introduction to Africa and the country of Botswana, a cutaway view of a termite mound, and a reproduction of an ancient rock painting. You can also get in-depth information on zebras, African elephants, and Botswana's antelope species. At the end of your Museum safari, you're bound to have a better appreciation for this unique African country and its spectacular wildlife.

This panorama shows the site depicted in the Savuti Crossroads diorama.

Sixties Safari and Optical Illusions

In 1969, the Museum sent an expedition to Botswana to document African plants and animals before their numbers or ranges declined any further. Our five-man field crew consisted of a curator and a preparator (both trained taxidermists), a photographer, an artist, and the Museum's assistant director. They were aided by Botswana's senior game warden, who took them to strategic spots for collecting big game, smaller mammals, and birds. In five months, the expedition members took hundreds of photographs, shot thousands of feet of motion-picture film, made hundreds of field sketches, and collected and prepared 100 cases of specimens for shipment back to Denver. Six staff members returned to Botswana in 1974 to collect foreground and reference materials for the dioramas. The hall opened in phases from 1976 to 1981. In 1998, it received a facelift in the form of cleaned and refurbished dioramas and new interpretive panels.

Exhibit makers dug into their bag of tricks for this hall's dioramas. A few of their secrets: In the Savuti Crossroads diorama, the shadows are dark-colored sand. The water is a clear polyester

Scenes from the field: local San people (left) and one of the 1969 expedition's camps

resin poured on top of a Mylar-covered board. The Mylar reflects the sky, giving the water its color. In the cheetah-impala diorama, a rod attaches the bounding impala to the back one. Exhibits staff created the swirling dust by spraying flat pieces of acetate plastic with mists of paint and installing the acetate in layers among the vegetation. Even inside the diorama, the acetate is nearly impossible to see.

Want to build a lifelike termite mound (above)? Make molds of real ones, as our staff did in Botswana in 1974.

fun facts

- According to the Museum's 1969 annual report, the tsetse fly and the mosquito "were the only very dangerous animals the [expedition members] had to face. There were a few brushes with lion and buffalo, and some staff members were chased by elephants, but nothing serious in outcome."
- Henry Ford II donated a Ford four-wheel-drive truck to the Museum for the 1969 Botswana expedition.
- The Savuti Crossroads diorama was enclosed with glass in 1993. It had been open since 1981. Staff wear a pair of zebra hoofprint shoes whenever they have to walk across the diorama.

South America

Meet the unique wildlife of our continental neighbor to the south.

Our South America hall touches on just three areas of the world's fourth largest continent. Even so, a stroll through this hall reveals that the wildlife look a bit different south of the equator (compared with North American species, that is).

Western Brazil's highlands, a region known as the Mato Grosso Plateau, serve as the setting for three dioramas. The largest illustrates the birds and mammals that frequent the edges of forests and savannas: howler monkeys; Brazilian tapirs *(above)*, with their short, trunklike noses; dog-size capybaras, the world's largest rodent; tiny Pampas deer; and a variety of colorful parrots and parakeets. The other two dioramas depict elusive black-maned wolves, an ostrichlike rhea with his brood of chicks, and two giant anteaters foraging for termites.

Three staff members collected these animals during the Museum's South American expedition of 1925–1926. When their Brazilian work was completed, they headed to southernmost Argentina, where, in the Patagonia region, they obtained the guanacos (a llama relative) now on display. Altogether the field party spent fourteen months away from Denver. In that time they collected 125 mammals and 750 birds for the Museum's exhibits and collections.

Brazilian tiger dance, 1925

The fifth diorama and an exhibit case highlight the Galápagos Islands, located about 600 miles (960 km) west of Ecuador. Observing the wildlife of the Galápagos in 1835 spurred Charles Darwin to develop his theory of evolution

Among South America's most famous animal inhabitants are capybaras (above) and the Galápagos tortoise.

by natural selection, which he published in 1859. In the exhibit case you can see some of the bird species, including Darwin's finches, that sparked a scientific revolution. The diorama features giant tortoises and land and marine iguanas from Santa Cruz Island. These specimens were obtained by the Museum's seven-man, two-month expedition to the Galápagos in 1960—101 years after Darwin forever changed the science of biology.

Official field vehicle, Argentina, 1926

- The emergency supplies for the 1925–1926 expedition included a bottle of iodine, a pair of tooth pullers, and a little quinine.

- Many of these specimens were originally installed in dioramas in the James (South) Wing. They were moved here in 1961. Three new or refurbished dioramas debuted in 1973.

Behind the Scenes

What Goes On

More than 650,000 objects (including drawers full of birds), several paleontologists, and even a live tarantula or two inhabit spaces not usually open to the public. Assembling the Tyrannosaurus rex, *1987 (left)*

Anthropology

Anthropologists working in museums study human beings by first analyzing the objects people have created. These objects had a "life" before they came to a museum. Someone used them for practical, decorative, or ceremonial purposes. Our curators try to reconstruct the lives of these past peoples—where they lived, how they survived, what they believed—by "reading" the objects.

The 50,000 objects in the Department of Anthropology's collections fall about equally into two subdivisions of anthropology: archaeology and ethnology. Archaeologists study peoples whose objects have been preserved in the earth. Ethnologists analyze and compare more recent cultures, including those of the present.

Archaeology

The Department of Anthropology's roots lie in the most famous archaeological discovery ever made by Museum staff: the 1926 finding of the Folsom point. Its existence provided the first evidence that humans had lived in North America since the end of the last Ice Age. Inspired by this and subsequent discoveries of mammoth fossils and projectile points at a site near Dent, Colorado, the Museum created a Department of Archaeology in 1935, with H. Marie Wormington as its first

Aerial photography without an airplane: documenting an archaeological site, Utah, 1948

A field crew searches for evidence of the first Americans in Alaska; a Clovis point (below).

curator. During her thirty-three-year tenure, Wormington sealed the Museum's international reputation in archaeology. She conducted excavations that documented several Paleoindian cultures, and her 1939 book *Ancient Man in North America* stood for decades as the definitive work on Paleoindian peoples.

The archaeology collections fall into two categories: amateur and systematic. The amateur collection consists of objects (mostly arrowheads) donated since the 1930s that are useful for educational programs and exhibits. The systematic collection provides the basis for archaeological research, publications, and exhibits. It contains everything uncovered at specific, methodically excavated sites: stone points and the flakes chipped off while making them, food refuse, animal remains, stone grinding tools. Artifacts from the Folsom and Dent sites are among the most famous in the collection.

In the late 1990s, the department resumed the search for the first Americans, concentrating its efforts on coastal areas of southeast Alaska. For years, the prevailing theory has been that humans came to North America from Asia over the Bering Land Bridge and then spread south across the continent. But in the late 1970s, a Canadian

A curator in Alaska; beads from Southeast Asia (right)

archaeologist proposed that humans using watercraft could have skirted the massive glaciers and found ice-free areas along the Northwest Coast as early as 16,000 to 14,000 years ago. The Museum's curator of archaeology teamed up with other scientists to search for evidence to support this theory. In 1996, they began excavating a cave on a remote island west of Ketchikan. Among their discoveries were a 9,200-year-old human jaw (the oldest human remains unearthed in Alaska or Canada) and a 10,300-year-old bone tool. Their studies may show that humans settled North America not from north to south but from west to east, arriving at the coast and then moving inland. Once again, Museum discoveries are revolutionizing North American archaeology.

Ethnology

Although the Museum has long accepted donations of ethnological materials, the collections got a jump start in 1968. Francis V. and Mary W. A. Crane closed their Southeast Museum of the North American Indian in Marathon, Florida, and donated its entire contents to the DMNS. The 14,000 artifacts represented years of collecting by the Cranes.

Thanks to the Cranes, the ethnology collections contain objects from every major American Indian tribe from Alaska to the Everglades. The collections also contain substantial material from Mexico and Central and South America. Some artifacts date back to the 1600s; others were made last year. Other components include a world comparative collection, with strong representation from southern Africa and Southeast Asia. The comparative collection allows researchers to seek out the differences and universal characteristics among the world's cultures.

Anthropology collections area

Ethnological objects fall into several categories: clothing, food containers, toys, transportation, communication, and ceremonial objects. These objects were made either for native use or for sale, a market that

Museum staff prepare Native American rattles and beadwork (inset); Kwakwa̱ka̱'wakw mask depicting Komokwa, the "Lord of the Undersea."

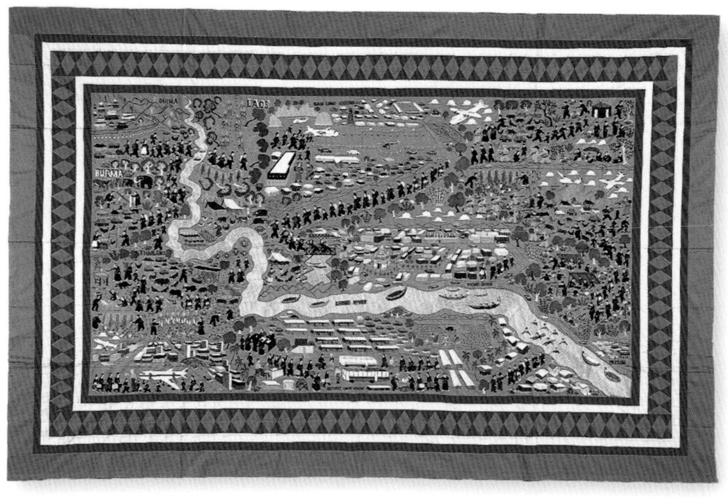

A Hmong story cloth depicts their journey from the war in Southeast Asia to America.

started at least a hundred years ago. Ethnologists usually prefer the former for research. Some of the most important objects in the collection show signs of wear and use—critical clues for the ethnologist.

Our curator of ethnology has documented the basketry, beadwork, and clothing of the Jicarilla Apache of northern New Mexico. Her long-term relationship with these people has allowed her to record the styles and techniques of individual craftswomen, ensuring that numerous details of their lives will be preserved. If the Jicarilla Apache culture fades over time, future generations will be able to recover lost elements of their heritage.

In 1973, the DMNS became one of the first museums in the nation to establish a Native American advisory group. This group of American Indians, all from the Denver area but representing tribes nationwide, has helped Museum staff develop most of our exhibits and programs about native peoples. This close working relationship has led to the annual Spring Buffalo Feast at the Museum, which honors Indian leaders and is attended by more than 1,000 Native Americans.

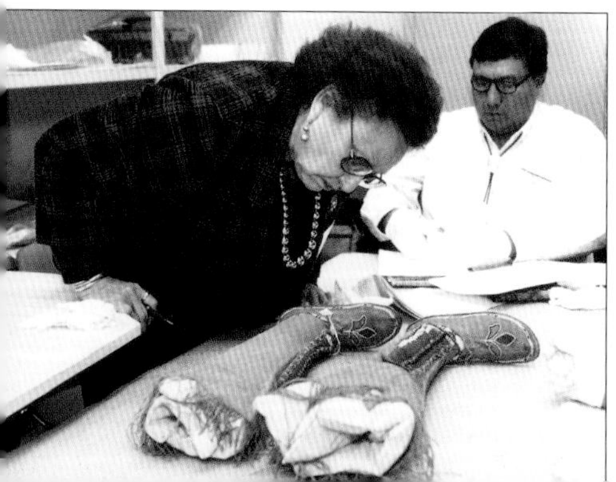

A Kiowa delegation examines artifacts during a NAGPRA consultation (left); an Oglala Sioux drum.

In recent years, much of the Anthropology Department's work has been driven by the Native American Graves Protection and Repatriation Act (NAGPRA). Passed by Congress in 1990, NAGPRA requires all museums receiving federal funds to repatriate, or return, if requested, certain types of American Indian materials. These include human remains, grave goods, and objects of cultural patrimony (objects owned by a community, not by an individual). Delegates from among the 420 tribes represented in our collections have visited the Museum to discuss any possible claims to these objects. These consultations provide tremendous opportunities for the tribes to learn more about their own cultures through the objects the Museum has preserved. In turn, the Museum learns more about each tribe's past and current ways of life. In numerous cases, NAGPRA has opened new lines of communication between the Museum and tribal peoples.

Native Americans preparing to dance at our annual Spring Buffalo Feast

- The Museum's collection of peace medals—medals given to American Indians by U.S. presidents as a symbol of peace—ranks among the best in the country.

- Heaviest object in the anthropology collections: Maya Stela 3, weighing in at approximately five tons. The ten-foot-tall slab of dolomitic limestone features hieroglyphs carved by the Mayas more than 1,350 years ago.

- Some members of our anthropology staff have been named honorary members of the Tlingit Killerwhale Clan and given Tlingit names.

Earth and Space Sciences

The Department of Earth and Space Sciences takes care of our oldest objects (4-billion-year-old rocks), reassembles our largest objects (dinosaurs), and covers the most territory geographically—from the center of the earth to the farthest reaches of outer space. The department includes the scientific disciplines of geology, paleontology, and astronomy and its related fields.

The terrestrial aspects of the department—geology and paleontology—go back to the early days of the institution: John F. Campion's collection of crystallized gold, and 800 fossils from Florissant, Colorado, collected by staff in 1915. The collections have grown substantially since then. Shelves and drawers now house 40,000 geological specimens and 84,000 fossils.

Geology

To gain a better understanding of Earth's history and the processes that have created the modern landscape, geologists study rocks. With rocks being made up of one or more minerals, our 21,000 mineral specimens provide geologists with literally tons of reference material. Not surprisingly, the Museum holds the world's largest collection of Colorado minerals. These minerals range from small, unassuming chunks of quartz to the spectacular Alma King, the world's largest crystal of rhodochrosite. The geology collections also house 15,800 micromounts, which are microscopic crystals of rare and unusual beauty.

In addition to minerals, the Museum houses some 480 meteorites, a collection largely built by honorary curator Harvey H. Nininger between 1931 and 1945. Nininger pioneered methods of locating meteorites based on eyewitness reports of fireballs in the night sky. Today our geologists work with a cadre of volunteers as

A curator shows copper minerals to a geology class; a selenite specimen in a protective mount (left).

unofficial investigators of such phenomena. Their goal is to inform area residents that a meteorite has fallen nearby. If someone finds it, we hope it will be donated to the Museum.

Another geological study area is Colorado's most visible but overlooked natural resource: building stones. Buildings in Denver and across the nation preserve evidence of the state's geologic past. By staring at a wall, a geologist can examine rhyolite that began as ash from a volcanic explosion 35 million years ago or sandstone that was a beach when Colorado had dinosaurs and a coastline 100 million years ago. The geology collections include samples of every Colorado stone used for buildings, specimens of interest to both scientists and historic preservationists.

Paleontology

Working in Denver is a real treat for a paleontologist, for the city lies on some of the most fossil-rich land in the world. Paleontologists are scientists who study fossils to learn about past life on Earth. They figure out what ancient animals and plants looked like, what their worlds were like, and how they changed over time.

Forty-one thousand animal fossils make up the vertebrate paleontology collections. Most of these fossils were discovered in the western United States, and some date back 500 million years. Fossilized bones form the backbone of the vertebrate collections, but also preserved are teeth, tracks, imprints of skin and feathers, and casts of fossils from other museums.

The vertebrate collections are best known for their mammals from the early Tertiary period of 65 to 35 million years ago, the time right after the dinosaurs went extinct. Among these specimens are the remains of entire herds of rhinoceros-like animals that once roamed North America. Dinosaurs represent another strength of the collections. The rocks of the 150-million-year-old Morrison Formation west of Denver preserved skeletons of numerous species, including *Diplodocus* and *Stegosaurus.*

The invertebrate collections are relatively small, containing some 9,000 specimens from all over the country. These specimens include clams, squid relatives, ammonites, trilobites, crinoids, and insects, to name a few of the groups represented.

Our paleobotany (fossil plant) collections rank among the best in the country. More than 34,000 specimens document the vegetation of Earth's past. Like their modern counterparts, fossil plants vary widely in size and shape, ranging from microscopic pollen grains to giant fossil logs. Most commonly preserved are petrified wood and fossil leaf imprints, but sometimes even waxy leaf cuticle—the dried leaf—survives. The large majority of our specimens are angiosperms, or flowering plants, from 95 to 35 million years ago, the 30 million years before and after the extinction of the dinosaurs. Our paleobotanist has documented that 80 percent of the plant species went extinct at the same time the dinosaurs did. This mass extinction provides convincing evidence that a major catastrophe occurred 65 million years ago—most likely, a huge asteroid striking the Earth.

Each summer the Museum sends staff and volunteers to the isolated reaches of Colorado, Wyoming, and North Dakota to collect more fossils. Research continues year-round as our paleontologists examine their finds closely. At some sites, such as one

Museum staff and volunteers dig for dinosaur fossils near Grand Junction; even the smallest fossils can hold important clues (inset); fossil leaves (opposite).

in northeastern Colorado called Bones Galore, crews carefully record the exact location of where each bone is found. When that information is entered into the computers of our Geographic Information System, scientists can create a three-dimensional image of the site inside the Museum. Our researchers dig up and study dinosaurs from the early Cretaceous period in Utah; Triassic-age fish, amphibians, and reptiles in western Colorado; and mammals from the Tertiary period in Colorado and Wyoming. With every discovery, the Museum's paleontologists add to our understanding of prehistoric life on this planet.

Plaster-coating fossils in Wyoming (left); unearthing an ammonite in Colorado (below); our paleobotany collections area (above).

Scanning the skies with the University of Denver's telescope

Space Science

Space science became the newest addition to the department in 1998 when the Museum hired its first curator of space science. She was joined two years later by our first space and planetary scientist. Their duties at the Museum include helping to develop space science exhibits and programming and building a collection from scratch—not of objects, but a digital one. The digital collection will contain images, data, video, audio, diagrams, and animation related to space science research—the same information with which astronomers work. Our scientists intend to document developments in space science and their impact on society as they unfold. With major discoveries being announced almost weekly, human perception of our place in the universe may change substantially within our lifetimes.

- The Lincoln Memorial in Washington, D.C., is made of 330-million-year-old Yule marble from Colorado. Our collection contains samples of the beautiful white building stone.
- A 1992 Museum discovery provided the first evidence that bony scutes covered stegosaurs' necks.
- Field crews have been known to munch on the abundant 67-million-year-old leaves preserved at a fossil site in North Dakota.
- Among the fossils discovered in the Denver area: parts of a *Tyrannosaurus rex* at a housing development in Littleton, and a dinosaur rib just behind the site of home plate at Coors Field.

Zoology

Zoology encompasses the study of every creature in the animal kingdom, but the Museum's Department of Zoology focuses its efforts on five groups of animals: birds, mammals, insects, spiders, and mollusks. Our zoology collections preserve more than 136,000 specimens from these groups. Each specimen helps document the variety of life, or biodiversity, found on Earth.

The Zoology Department can trace its roots back to the Museum's founding, with two of our first three collections being zoological ones. Since 1908, zoological specimens have been the centerpieces of our popular exhibits.

Ornithology

Our ornithological, or bird, collection contains some 50,000 specimens, its greatest strength being birds from the Rocky Mountains and Great Plains. Our collection also houses numerous species from around the world, thanks to Museum expeditions over the years. Other collection highlights include more than 7,000 sets of eggs, 500 nests, and specimens of six extinct species.

Museums preserve most birds as study skins. Used almost exclusively for research, a study skin is a skin stuffed with cotton and laid out flat so that many will fit safely in each storage cabinet drawer. The skull, leg, and wing bones are left inside. In other cases, the bird's entire skeleton is preserved. For a robin-size bird, it takes a preparator about an hour to remove most of the tissue from the bones. Then a colony of dermestid beetles eats off any remaining flesh, just as it would in nature. After a week or two among the dermestids, the bones are ready to become part of the collections.

Birds (and other animals) in the collections serve a variety of purposes. Law enforcement officials compare confiscated items, such as eagle feathers or exotic fur coats, to Museum specimens to verify their identity. Artists use specimens as references for field guide illustrations. And of course, scientists use the specimens for research.

Mammalogy

The Museum's mammal collection holds 10,000 specimens, primarily species from Colorado and the surrounding states, but also from such faraway places as Australia and Africa. The specimens are preserved much the same as the birds: as study skins, skeletal material, and taxidermy mounts. For larger mammals, however, tanned hides are kept instead of study skins; they're easier to store that way.

With mammals, both the skin and the complete skeleton can be preserved. The curator of mammalogy has sent frozen tissue samples to the Museum of Texas Tech University for storage. Doing so provides future researchers with tissue samples for DNA analysis and other studies. Such partnerships ensure that future scientists will be able to learn as much as possible from every new specimen, perhaps using techniques we can't even imagine today.

Entomology and Arachnology

Entomology and arachnology both involve arthropods, or animals with jointed legs and external skeletons. Entomology is the study of insects—arthropods with three body segments, a single pair of antennae, and six legs. Arachnology is the study of spiders—arthropods with two body segments, no antennae, and eight legs.

By entomologists' standards, ours is a relatively small insect collection, with

From top: study skin of a ground squirrel; rearticulated grey fox skeleton; common Colorado spider; searching for spiders

Colorado Spider Survey volunteers (right) collect the eight-legged creatures and then place them in vials of ethanol.

Students watch for hawks on Dinosaur Ridge; ferruginous hawk (below).

only 60,000 specimens. Unlike a mammal or bird, an insect requires very little preparation to become part of the collection—just a pin placed through its right side and an identification tag (with very tiny writing) pressed into a foam base. Insects are also easier to collect. If you've spent any time outdoors, you know how abundant they are.

The spider collection houses 7,000 small vials of spiders preserved in ethanol. Each vial holds from one to fifty spiders. This, too, is a small collection, but with a major research effort under way, it will likely triple in size. In 1999, the Colorado Spider Survey was initiated to gather information on which species live in the state. Staff and trained volunteers have fanned out to collect spiders from all of Colorado's varied ecosystems. It's almost certain that species new to science will be discovered.

The curator of entomology and arachnology also assumes responsibility for the 16,000 lots of shells in the conchology collection. Since its inception, the shell collection has been curated primarily by volunteers. Like most collections, only a tiny portion is on exhibit—less than one percent.

Zoological Research and Collections

Since 1990, the Department of Zoology has devoted most of its fieldwork to monitoring the "health" of various ecosystems and animal populations. Study sites have included the Rocky Mountain Arsenal near Denver International Airport, the Dinosaur Ridge Raptor Migration Station west of Denver, and the South Platte River corridor through Denver. The department has been engaged in a

Our zoologists document wildlife along the South Platte River; Ord's kangaroo rat (below).

study of the Comanche National Grassland in southeastern Colorado. Staff, interns (including high school students), and volunteers band hawks; monitor raptor nests and small rodent and rabbit populations; record weather conditions; and make detailed maps of vegetation, land use, and nesting sites using our computerized Geographic Information System. They hope to gain new insights into how a shortgrass prairie ecosystem works—how a change in one plant or animal species affects the others.

Studies like these account for just a few additions to our collections each year. For both ethical and economic reasons, museums no longer undertake major collecting expeditions like the ones that obtained the animals for our dioramas. Collecting is done only when necessary and only with a permit from a government agency. The majority of additions now are road-killed mammals or window-killed birds brought in by the public, donations of private arthropod or shell collections, or dead animals donated by government agencies or zoos.

People often ask why we collect more than one specimen of each species. Museums do so because species vary as much in their appearance as humans do. One individual cannot represent its entire species. Moreover, animals change both during their lifetime and over hundreds of years. To get a complete picture, researchers need to examine many individuals of different ages, from various places, collected in all four seasons over many years.

The specimens in our zoology collections are irreplaceable treasures. By studying them, we can better understand their living relatives' lifestyles—knowledge that enables us to make informed decisions about our stewardship of the living universe.

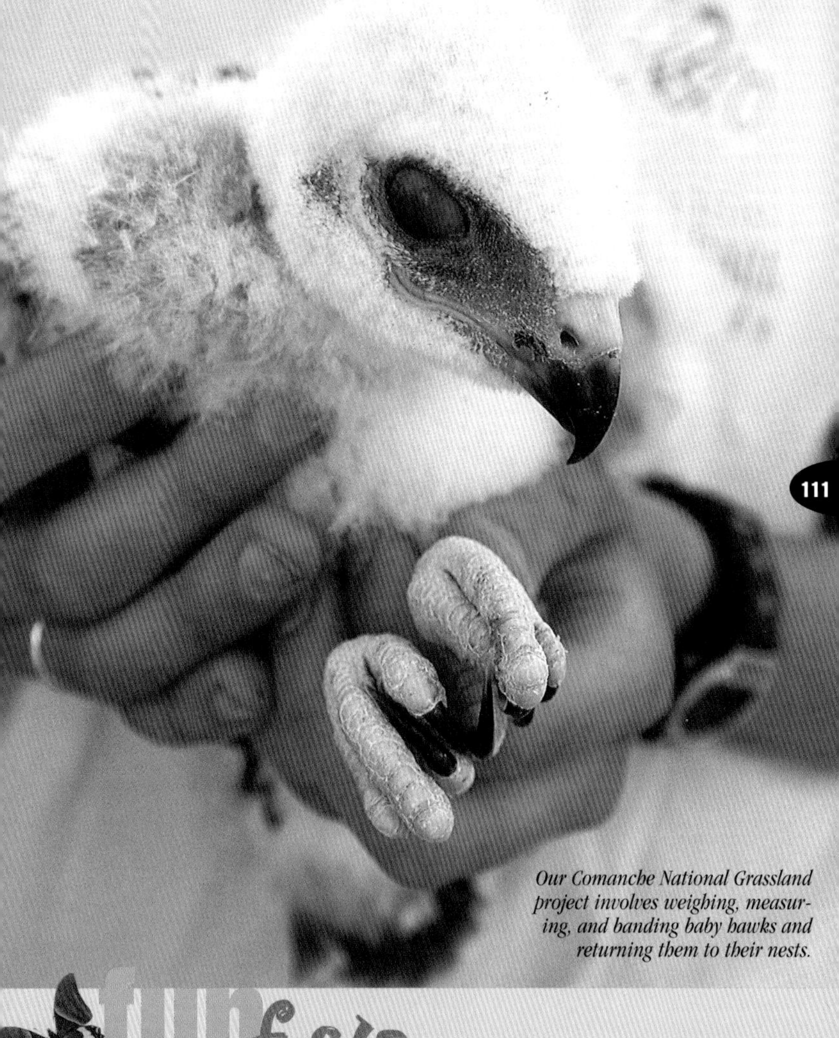

Our Comanche National Grassland project involves weighing, measuring, and banding baby hawks and returning them to their nests.

fun facts

- A large refrigerator-size cabinet housing extinct and type specimens is the Museum's only storage cabinet on wheels. (A type specimen is the individual specimen on which a scientist based the description of a new species.) In an emergency, these invaluable specimens would be hustled to safety.
- Our conchology collection includes several shells donated by the late Raymond Burr, the actor of *Perry Mason* and *Ironside* fame.
- Among the oldest objects in the zoology collections: eggs of *Aepyornis,* a gigantic flightless bird of Madagascar that went extinct in the 1600s or 1700s.

Education Collections

If you get the chance to hold a dinosaur bone or play an African drum during your visit, you've discovered our education collections. The Museum keeps these objects so that they can be touched, held, and used.

Most objects in the education collections are "the real thing," just like the ones in the research collections. The 30,000 artifacts include mounted mammals and birds, skins and skeletons, fossils, rocks, minerals, clothing and toys from around the world, and much more. Many lack information about where or when they were found or who made them, making them ill-suited for scientific research. The education collections also are broader in scope than the research collections, primarily because our educational programs cover broader topics. Replicas and reproductions, such as modern arrowheads made using ancient techniques, find a home in the education collections, too.

Since 1970, education collection objects have shown up in an amazing number of places: touch carts, discovery centers, classes for schoolchildren, weekend and summer workshops, Hall of Life classes, outreach programs. With some objects being handled by up to 800 people a day, it's impossible to keep them in pristine condition forever. Staff and volunteers try to make each object last as long as possible through gentle handling and every glue known to the museum profession. Despite their best efforts, many objects eventually wear out and have to be deaccessioned, or retired. Adding objects to the collections has become a never-ending job. Everyone involved wants to ensure that children fifty years from now have the chance to pet a polar bear, piece together a 50-million-year-old turtle shell, or climb inside a tipi.

Storage area packed with touchable objects

EDUCATION

Conservation

You might think that once an object joins our collections, it's preserved forever. Long-term preservation is certainly our goal. As years pass, however, many objects deteriorate naturally even under the best circumstances. Destructive forces can speed the process. Various insects sneak into the building and try to snack on tasty hides, fur, and feathers. Colorado's low humidity makes some objects brittle, especially in winter. Light fades textiles, skins, furs, feathers, and dyes.

A conservator injects adhesives into an ancient Egyptian coffin to keep its paint layer from falling off.

Since 1990, the Department of Conservation has waged a tireless battle to keep the destructive forces at bay and to slow the deterioration process. Most of their efforts go into preventive conservation—trying to avoid damage instead of repairing it. Our conservators monitor temperature and relative humidity throughout the Museum, controlling these factors as much as possible to provide a stable environment for the objects. Ultraviolet filters on fluorescent lights and low light levels slow the fading process, and the conservators watch like hawks for insects or other pests inside dioramas and storage areas. You might notice some of their equipment tucked into corners of exhibits. Small boxes with dials monitor the climate inside cases; strips of graduated blue fabric help measure fading; and insect traps snare illicit bugs.

Conservation staff helped rehouse several collections during the 1990s, including kachina dolls, masks, baskets, and minerals. These projects involved moving hundreds of artifacts from crowded spaces on wooden shelves to ample homes in secure, state-of-the-art metal cabinets. Selected objects received customized storage mounts that support and protect the artifacts and reduce the risk of accidental damage from handling.

A mask is sealed in a plastic bag to create an airtight environment.

Occasionally objects must be repaired or stabilized. For example, before *Egyptian Mummies* opened in 1998, conservators wrapped one more layer of material around the "poor woman's mummy"—a fine, nylon netting that holds her linen wrappings in place. Written records and photographs document every procedure. With such measures and a gentle touch, our Conservation staff helps keep every object in good condition for as long as humanly possible.

A kachina doll is examined for signs of damage or insect infestation.

Library/Archives

Library

Unbeknownst to many, the Museum has its own library, which is open to the public. Started in 1920, the Library now houses more than 32,000 books and periodicals. These volumes span all of the fields in which the Museum specializes—anthropology, geology, health science, paleontology, space science, and zoology—as well as museum studies. Within these topics, there's something for just about everyone, from children to scholars. A rare book collection preserves such treasures as late eighteenth-century reports of Captain James Cook's voyages.

All you need to check out a book is a valid Colorado library card. Anyone with Internet access can search the Library's catalog. Look for it on the Museum's Web site at www.dmns.org.

Among the stacks are reference books, journals, children's books, and helpful staff.

Boxes filled with prints, slides, and transparencies line the walls of Photo Archives.

Archives

The Museum's archivist oversees a collection of materials that records the history of the institution. The preserved materials include minutes of board meetings, field notes, letters, oral histories on audiotape, building plans, and personal papers. Together they fill up 1,200 cubic feet (34 cubic meters) of space behind several dioramas. Researchers can consult the scraps of manila wrapping paper on which Edwin Carter recorded specimen data in the late 1800s or read the correspondence relating to our 1926 discovery of the Folsom point. Such careful documentation adds substantial scientific value to the Museum's collections.

An account of Captain Cook's voyages, published in 1777

Photo Archives

Museum staff have been taking photographs and shooting motion pictures for most of the institution's history. Photo Archives preserves more than 300,000 of these images in such diverse formats as lantern slides, black-and-white prints, color slides, 16mm motion-picture film, and video. They illustrate the evolution of our building and exhibits, artifacts in our collections, fieldwork, and the natural world. Photo Archives also holds donated collections, such as Jesse H. Bratley's photographs of life on American Indian reservations between 1895 and 1912.

Both the archives and the photo archives are available to the public by appointment.

Clockwise from left: Snowy egret; Governor's Palace, Djibouti, French Somaliland, 1926; Buckskin Charlie, a Ute Indian, 1905; five men, Canton, China, ca. 1890–1910; Sioux children on their first day of school, 1898

Making Exhibits

Most people come to the Museum to see our exhibits. What many remember are our incredible dioramas. Each one carefully blends science and art, reproducing the natural world as accurately and realistically as possible.

Bringing Nature Inside

Building each diorama involved years of work. Once a theme had been selected for a new hall—for example, Alaskan mammals—Museum staff traveled to the chosen state or country for weeks of research and fieldwork. They selected a specific site for each diorama to depict. Zoologists and taxidermists collected specimens, taking detailed notes and measurements. Exhibits staff sketched and collected vegetation and made molds of trees and rocks. Background artists took photographs and painted studies of the landscape.

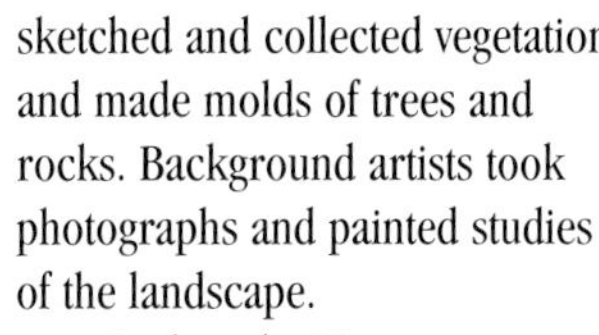

Back at the Museum, re-creating nature began. The taxidermists transformed collected specimens into a diorama's centerpieces. Mannequins, custom-made for each specimen, froze the animals in the middle of natural movements. Then the skins or tanned hides were sewn or glued onto the mannequins. Final cosmetic touches—adding glass

Fieldwork for Montague Island diorama, 1978

Clockwise from top: Painting a dinosaur mural; painting the Kansas Coastline background; preparing albatross specimens; making aspen branches

"He draws on walls, and nobody stops him" is one five-year-old's definition of a staff artist's job; Dall's sheep (insets): mannequin and finished mounts.

eyes, waxing the hair, arranging feathers, painting exposed flesh—made the finished mounts look as lifelike as possible.

The foregrounds—the plants and rocks on the diorama's floor—required much tedious effort. Dried grasses, woody shrubs, ferns, and conifers were preserved and installed in dioramas; everything else had to be made from scratch. Every leaf, flower, and blade of green grass was cut out of vinyl or crepe paper or wax, painstakingly assembled with wire and glue, and painted by hand. Using molds from the field, trees and rocks were made of plaster, concrete, or fiberglass and then skillfully painted to match the originals. Paints were mixed inside the dioramas to ensure that colors look realistic under the filtered fluorescent lights.

The paintings that grace the curved, domed backgrounds of our dioramas are truly works of art, each the equivalent of up to 1,000 easel-size paintings. The artists who created them all had different styles and techniques. One artist, responsible for twenty-eight of our 100 dioramas, could start painting on one side and work his way around—without sketching in the overall perspective! Another longtime staff artist pioneered projecting photographs of the site onto the walls, using up to ten slide projectors. It took him eight months to three years to complete each background. Yet, he became so adept at using a twelve-foot-long (4-m) pole *(left)*—a roller on one end, an air brush on the other—that he could paint a sky in three days. The most difficult part of any diorama was the tie-in, the point at which the painted background meets the plants and rocks of the foreground. It's rarely easy to see where one stops and the other begins—a testament to their collective artistry.

Restoring a foreground plant means repainting every leaf by hand.

These processes apply mostly to wildlife dioramas, but similar methods created the dioramas in North American Indian Cultures, Gems and Minerals, and *Prehistoric Journey.* A small exhibit in North American Wildlife on the second floor illustrates the techniques. No matter the hall, the end result is the same: A moment in time at a particular place—a season, a time of day, a real-life event—has been captured for millions to see and enjoy.

Creating an Experience

Dioramas have been the Museum's mainstay for decades, but today our exhibitions incorporate elements unimagined not long ago—videos, computer interactives, multimedia presentations. Exhibits Division staff team up with curators and educators to create these fun, memorable, educational experiences for our visitors. Developers write scripts, and designers use computers to create floor plans, case layouts, and graphic panels. Skilled craftspeople build cases and silk-screen graphics onto panels. Along the way, evaluators ask visitors for feedback on content issues and prototypes, input that helps hone the final product. It literally takes an army of talented people to create an exhibition. Thanks to their efforts, six Museum exhibitions have been awarded national honors since 1992, continuing our long-standing tradition of producing high-quality exhibits.

Creating Prehistoric Journey *included welding supports for dinosaur skeletons (left) and installing graphic panels.*

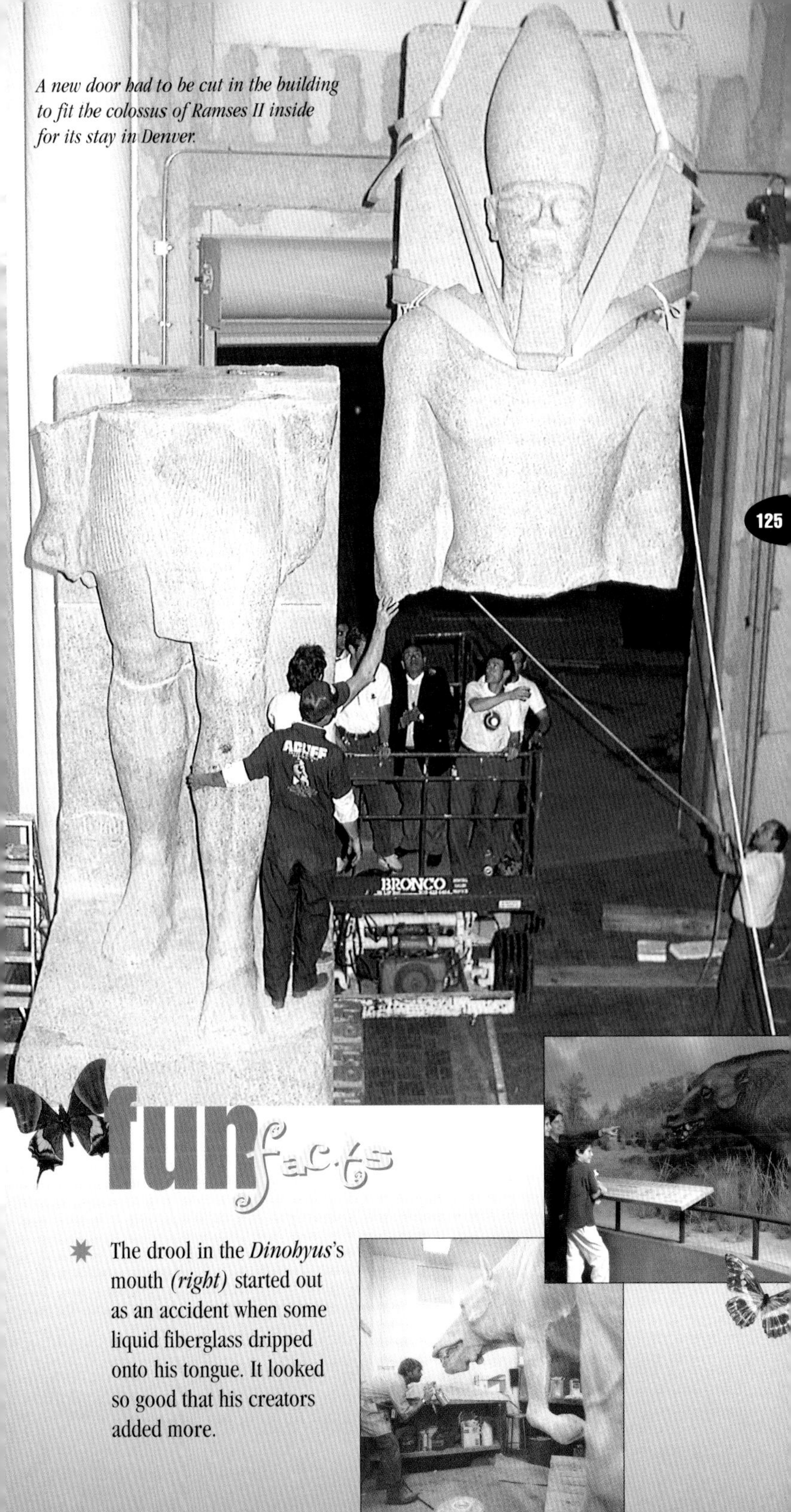

A new door had to be cut in the building to fit the colossus of Ramses II inside for its stay in Denver.

fun facts

- The drool in the *Dinohyus*'s mouth *(right)* started out as an accident when some liquid fiberglass dripped onto his tongue. It looked so good that his creators added more.

Volunteers

The Denver Museum of Nature and Science boasts the largest active volunteer corps of any natural history museum in the country. Each year, some 1,300 to 2,000 people donate their time and talents to almost every department in the Museum. Volunteers greet visitors, serve as tour guides, staff touch carts, assist with fieldwork, help care for collections, and work on exhibits. Chances are you'll interact with at least one of these dedicated people during a Museum visit.

Helping visitors explore fossils

Our volunteers range in age from 6 to 99, but the vast majority are retired. They come to the Museum for the opportunity to learn while doing something interesting and worthwhile. Some have been doing so for more than twenty-five years. Each volunteer receives both formal and on-the-job training, and most volunteers work directly with visitors or right alongside staff members. The perks include free admission to the Museum, IMAX, and various programs; discounts on food, merchandise, and memberships; and annual recognition events.

Volunteers have been a vital part of the Museum's operations since its inception. John T. Mason ran the Museum on a volunteer basis for its first ten years. From 1911 to 1983, honorary curators donated their expertise in various fields, including geology, meteorites, conchology, and botany. In 1972, the Junior League of Denver and Museum staff established a formal volunteer program, and in the

Volunteers interview visitors (top), take school groups on tours (above), and prepare fossils.

late 1980s, hundreds of new volunteers signed on to help with blockbuster exhibitions such as *Ramses II.* Volunteers administered the program until 1988, when the Museum first hired staff to coordinate volunteer activities.

Volunteers have outnumbered staff almost three to one, and their contribution to the Museum's work is staggering. Volunteers give more than 150,000 hours of their time annually. That's the equivalent of seventy-five full-time staff members. We couldn't open our doors and provide visitors with a high-quality experience without the enthusiastic commitment of our volunteers.

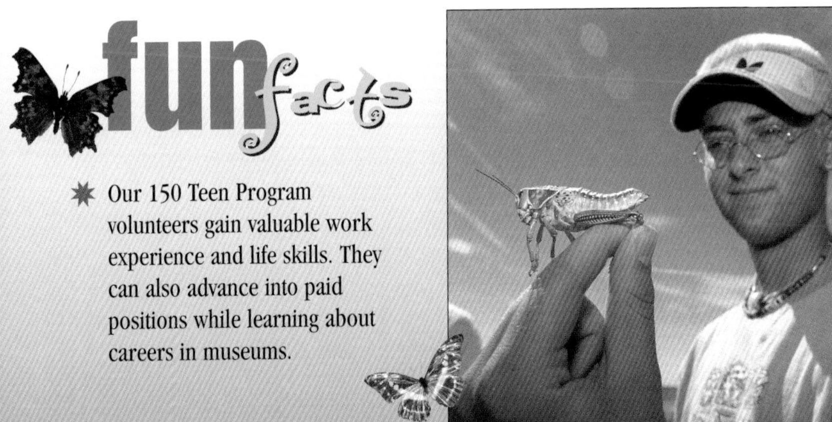

fun facts

- Our 150 Teen Program volunteers gain valuable work experience and life skills. They can also advance into paid positions while learning about careers in museums.

Making Learning Fun

Although valuable in their own right, museum objects take on a new life when people get a chance to connect with them—to see or touch something really old, unique, beautiful, or from another culture. Providing such opportunities is the mission of the Museum's Education Division. Through a variety of object-based programs, our educators help people of all ages discover the world around them—and have a good time in the process!

For the Younger Set

Many kids consider a trip to the Museum a highlight of their year. To ensure that it is, the Museum has developed numerous programs for children, each designed to stimulate curiosity and instill a sense of wonder. More than 500,000 children attend programs here each year.

To explore the Museum's exhibits, school groups can take a tour led by a trained volunteer. The volunteer brings along a basket of objects related to the tour's theme, be it Colorado treasures or animals of the world. Other school groups opt for classroom programs. Taught by experienced staff, Museum Preschool Adventures and Classroom Adventures use hands-on activities and art projects to explore cultural and natural history in depth. Topics range from "Fur, Feathers, and Fins" to "West African Mask Making." The Hall of Life offers similar classes in health sciences. Students can learn about "Germ-Mania" or "You've Got Guts" or dissect a frog in a learning lab. School and youth groups can even spend the night in the Museum at one of our "camp-ins."

School groups also come to the Museum to see scientific research in action. Through the magic of satellite television, the JASON Project transports students to a different spot each spring—from the bottom of the Mediterranean to the treetops of the Amazon rainforest. During these two weeks, students can peer over researchers' shoulders, ask questions, and pilot remote cameras or vehicles. A select few travel with the scientists and participate in the nationwide broadcasts.

When school's not in session, children can explore natural history at a weekend or summer workshop. These programs are wildly popular with both parents and kids. Children's workshop participants handle Museum objects, create imaginative crafts, and tour the Museum. Hall of Life workshops offer kids the chance to make healthy snacks or become a junior surgeon. Our Treasure House program helps preschoolers discover the natural world on their own (with an instructor, of course), whereas Parent-Child Workshops allow families to explore together.

We also offer workshops for teachers. These sessions provide tools for educators so that they can help their students excel and enjoy learning.

Exploring the world: camp-ins, classes, and family activities

For the Young at Heart

The Museum advocates lifelong learning, believing you're never too old to explore the world around you. Consequently, our Adult Programs staff schedules nearly a hundred lectures and classes each year to cater to interests across the scientific and cultural spectrum. All programs are open to the public, but Museum members get the first chance to register.

Amateur paleontologists-in-training attend class in the field.

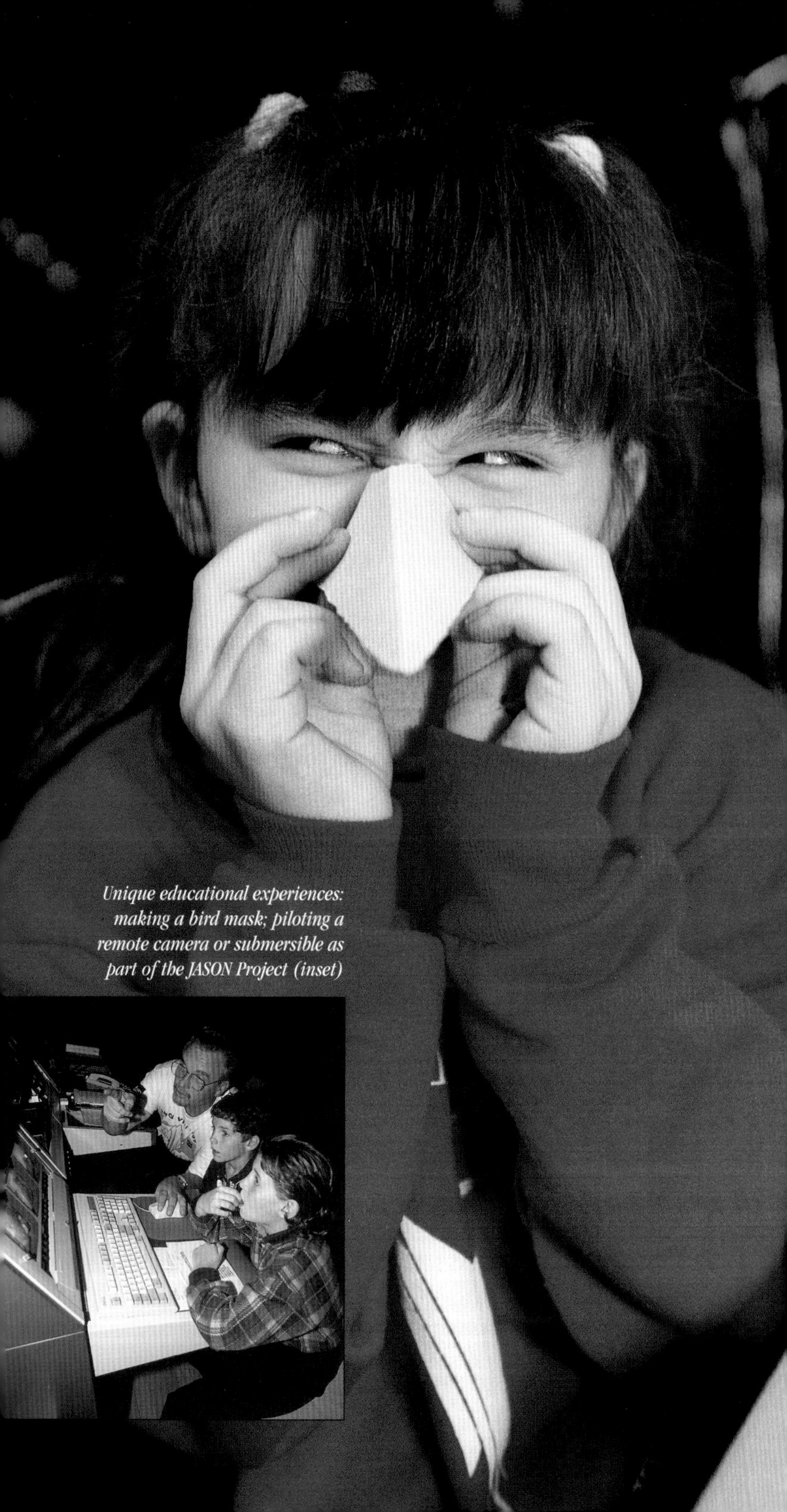

Unique educational experiences: making a bird mask; piloting a remote camera or submersible as part of the JASON Project (inset)

Classes and activities at the Museum can teach you how to draw or make an African Kufi hat (right).

For those who want to invest only an evening on a topic, lectures are the way to go. A typical month's lineup might include talks on an Egyptian pharaoh, the history of the universe, or the extinction of Ice Age mammals. The lecturers are a mix of Museum staff and local or visiting scholars. Past speakers have included such renowned scientists and explorers as Jane Goodall, Stephen Jay Gould, Richard Leakey, and Sir Edmund Hillary.

People who want to get deeper into a subject can take multi-session classes. Topics range from identifying spiders or rocks to drawing dinosaurs to studying American Indian baskets. The classes frequently involve hands-on experience with Museum objects, student participation, and weekend field trips—but no tests.

The most intensive set of classes offered is our Certification in Paleontology Program. Once participants complete seven required courses, they are certified to help staff collect fossils or to prepare specimens in the fossil lab. Several program graduates have even presented original research at meetings of paleontologists. The program has become a national model for continuing education in museums.

Exploring Beyond the Walls

The Museum's educational efforts aren't confined inside the building. Outreach programs and various publications take Museum experiences to audiences all over Denver, throughout Colorado and nearby states, and even across the nation.

We Deliver

Our Worlds of Wonder (WOW) Van takes tabletop exhibits, demonstration programs, and a portable planetarium to schools whose students can't make it to the Museum. The WOW Van often spends a week away from Denver, visiting schools in distant corners of Colorado or Wyoming. The traveling instructors present assemblies to entire schools or lead hands-on activities with small groups of students. Hall of Life staff also travel around the state, presenting the same classes and learning labs they teach at the Museum—frogs and sheep hearts included.

WOW Van: The Museum hits the road.

Outreach programs target other groups as well. Hall of Life staff set up health fairs for businesses and community events. Interactive learning tables, detailed models, and a professional health educator provide information and answer questions about nutrition, organ transplants, or the effects of smoking. Volunteers present programs at local nursing homes and senior centers. The slides and artifacts often evoke long-lost memories for the residents.

Outreach programs touch people of all ages, from face-painting for youngsters at community festivals to taking objects to nursing home residents (inset).

Tour participants see the wildlife (above) and meet the people (left) of Tanzania.

Seeing the Sights

Although the Museum makes every effort to bring the world to Denver, sometimes it's better to take people to see the world for themselves. With this philosophy in mind, the Museum organizes three to five day-trips a week to places within an hour or two of Denver. Participants can go bird-watching, visit wildlife refuges, or tour local research facilities.

Our domestic and international travel programs give people the chance to experience exotic places—and to really learn about their surroundings. A study leader, usually one of our curators or educators, accompanies most tours. The forty destinations each year include Alaska, Antarctica, and everywhere in between. Travelers can study the geology of the San Juan River by raft, explore the Arctic aboard a Russian icebreaker, stay in a Navajo hogan, photograph polar bears from a tundra crawler, or witness a solar eclipse in Madagascar. There's an itinerary to suit almost every interest and budget.

Read All About It

The printed page represents yet another medium with which the Museum reaches its audiences. Our members receive publications that keep them informed of current research projects, provide behind-the-scenes glimpses of exhibitions and programs, and list the numerous events and programs scheduled in the months ahead.

The Museum also publishes award-winning books for a wide range of audiences—from children to the general public to scholars. Some books, such as *Prehistoric Journey: A History of*

Since 1990, the Museum has published more than forty books on a variety of natural history topics.

Life on Earth and *Explore Colorado: A Naturalist's Notebook,* allow you to take part of the Museum home with you, whereas others help you explore new worlds from the comfort of your armchair. Our curators and educators review every word and illustration for accuracy on topics ranging from wildlife to world cultures. DMNS Press books are available at the Museum Shop or from your local bookseller.

- Television arrived in Denver in 1953. In 1954, the Museum produced its first of many TV shows in collaboration with local stations. Shown here is an early 1960s broadcast from the unfinished Campbell Island diorama.

The Future

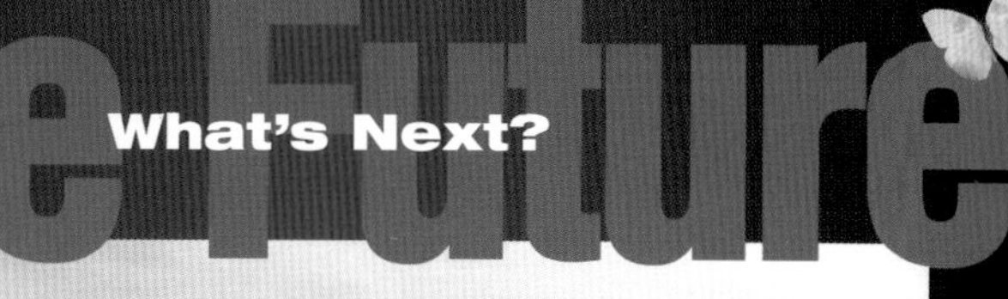

What's Next?

"A museum of natural history is never finished."

—John F. Campion, speaking at the Museum's opening exercises, July 1, 1908

As we explore the world around us, our collections will grow, and our exhibits and programs will continue to offer opportunities for discovery.

We'll keep digging for knowledge until future generations of staff, volunteers, and visitors take over the search. The Museum will always be a work in progress.

Credits
Photography & Illustration

Photographers: DMNS Photo Archives, Rick Wicker, Annette Slade, Gary D. Hall, Richard Stum, Nancy K. Jenkins, David McGrath, David Baysinger, Lance Carpenter, Kirk Johnson, Jack Murphy, Eric Parrish, David Shrader, Salle Tulchin, Betsy Webb

vi top left, 109 bottom © Buzz Morrison
9 top right © Denver Public Library Western History Collection, F-11716 by E. C. Peabody
19 bottom left C. R. O'Dell and S. K. Wong (Rice Univ.) and NASA
22 bottom © Denver Public Library Western History Collection, X-17659
26 top, 27 bottom courtesy NASA
27 top J. P. Harrington and K. J. Borkowski (Univ. of Maryland) and NASA
28 top Phillip James (Univ. of Toledo), Steven Lee (Univ. of Colorado), and NASA
29 background R. Williams (STScI), HDF South Team, and NASA
29 inset Bruce Balick (Univ. of Washington), Vincent Icke (Leiden Univ.), Garrett Mellema (Stockholm Univ.), and NASA
30 background Jeff Hester and Paul Scowen (Arizona State Univ.) and NASA
31 top Reta Beebe (New Mexico State Univ.), D. Gilmore and L. Bergeron (STScI), and NASA
64 © MacGillivray Freeman Films
67 top right © University of Colorado Health Sciences Center, Center for Human Simulation
76 Lucy reconstruction by John Gurche
83 center right © Smithsonian Institution Archives, Record Unit 7006, Alexander Wetmore Papers, Negative #1863

DENVER MUSEUM OF
NATURE & SCIENCE™ | *Press*